SONNY MONTGOMERY

Sonny Montgomery

THE VETERAN'S CHAMPION

G. V. "Sonny" Montgomery
with Michael B. Ballard and Craig S. Piper

Published by Mississippi State University Libraries

Distributed by University Press of Mississippi

www.upress.state.ms.us

The University Press of Mississippi
is a member of the Association of American University Presses.

Copyright © 2003 by Mississippi State University Libraries
All rights reserved
Manufactured in the United States of America
Photographs courtesy of the G.V. "Sonny" Montgomery Collection,
Congressional and Political Research Center, Mississippi State University
Libraries

04 03   2 1

Library of Congress Cataloging-in-Publication Data

Montgomery, G. V. (Gillespie V.)
 Sonny Montgomery : the veteran's champion / G. V. "Sonny"
Montgomery ; with Michael B. Ballard and Craig S. Piper.
p. cm.
Includes index.
ISBN 1-57806-554-2 (cloth : alk. paper)
 1. Montgomery, G. V. (Gillespie V.) 2. Legislators—United
States—Biography. 3. United States. Congress. House—
Biography. I. Ballard, Michael B. II. Piper, Craig S. III. Title.

E840.8.M665A3 2003
328.73'092—dc21   2002154359

British Library Cataloging-in-Publication Data available

CONTENTS

FOREWORD

Sonny Montgomery remains one of my closest personal friends. While I served in Congress and after that in the Executive Branch of government, Sonny remained a close confidant, a man whose judgment I always trusted, a man whose friendship gave me comfort when the going got tough.

Sonny is a Democrat. I am a Republican. But party never divided us. Oh, there may have been certain votes where each party had to maintain party discipline; but for the most part I could count on Congressman Montgomery's vote on key issues, and when it came to matters affecting our vital national security and matters of war and peace, we stood as one.

The entire Bush family will always be grateful to Congressman Gillespie Montgomery. Two Presidents Bush of the United States will remain ever grateful to him for his steadfast and loyal support.

I am sure the memoirs of this outstanding leader will be a must read for students at MSU and across the country who are interested in good government and who believe as I do that loyalty and friendships are much of what life should be about.

And, oh yes, who said, "Nice guys finish last"? Sonny Montgomery proves nice guys can finish first, while serving their country with honor.

GEORGE H. W. BUSH
41st President of the United States

I

The Early Years

No matter how far I have traveled, how many heads of state I've met, or how many presidents I've dined with, my roots remain in the Magnolia State—Mississippi. As you will see, my early childhood may not have been the easiest, but my generous family and friends offered the love and support that every young boy needs to become a happy, involved, and well-adjusted citizen. These early memories of my life may be far in the past, but they shaped me and influenced who I am today.

I was born in Meridian, Mississippi, on August 5, 1920, at Rush Hospital to Gillespie and Emily Montgomery. Since I was named after my father, my nickname quickly became "Sonny." I was born into a family that was deeply rooted in Mississippi. My father hailed from Starkville, and my grandfather was the son of Colonel W. B. Montgomery, one of the founders of Mississippi A&M, now Mississippi State University. This family tie is often referred to as the "Montgomery Connection" in and around Starkville. Another tie I have to Starkville is the Gillespie name, from my great-grandmother. My grandmother on my father's side was a Prowell from West Point. My Meridian roots come from my grandfather Montgomery's move to the central Mississippi town from Starkville after he opened a stockyard during the early 1900s.

My father returned to Starkville and attended A&M for one year. He then moved back to Meridian, where he met my mother, Emily Jones. My father was about twenty-two and my mother was twenty when they married. My father was in the gasoline and oil wholesale business, but any advancement in his profession was put on hold when he became infected with tuberculosis. Apparently, Grandfather Montgomery had purchased a home that was previously inhabited by persons infected with TB. Consequently, shortly after moving into the home, my father, aunt, and uncle contracted the disease.

Because of my father's condition, we moved to Phoenix, Arizona, shortly after I was born. We stayed in Phoenix for a couple of years, hoping that the dry climate would cure my father's ailment. Thinking he was cured, the whole family moved back to Meridian when I was about two and a half years old. My father then moved us to Memphis, Tennessee, and found his niche selling fuel tank cars to gasoline retailers throughout the United States.

But my father's success would be short-lived. His TB returned, and we moved back to Meridian. When I was ten, my father succumbed to the disease that had been with him for a decade. After his passing, we remained in Meridian, and about two years later, my mother married a man named James Tims, a Meridian oil broker.

I had seen many changes and experienced a couple of bumps in the road during my first ten years of life. Now, as the early 1930s approached, Mississippi and the rest of the country experienced a terrible depression. Economic circumstances being what they were, my family had to follow the jobs. For me this meant living in different places and attending different schools throughout my youth. I attended Marion Park Public School and Kate Griffin Junior High in Meridian. While in junior high, I played sports and was captain of the football team. I made some great friends in Meridian while growing up who are still living and remain close friends. For example, Preston "Pep" Bennett, a retired cotton farmer who now lives in Clarksdale, is still a dear friend, and I talk to him every Sunday evening. Nat I. Washburn Jr. and Thomas H. Hampton were also great friends, and I still keep in touch with them on a regular basis. Another great friend was Austin Ferrell of Hattiesburg, who just recently died. My family moved to Hattiesburg right after I finished junior high school, where my stepfather managed a W.P.A. office, and I switched schools again.

Hearing that the family was struggling and moving frequently, my wealthy great-aunt Mrs. J. W. (Alice) Pope, in Starkville came to our aid. My aunt Alice was well respected in the community, and her daughter, Ann Pope, married Dr. C. B. Mitchell, the chief physician at Mississippi State College. Nonetheless, my aunt offered to send me to McCallie School, a military boarding school in Chattanooga, Tennessee, where I completed the tenth, eleventh, and twelfth grades. While at McCallie I learned how to study and take care of myself, as we lived in dormitories on campus. McCallie's influence on my life was great; Dr. J. P. McCallie, Spencer McCallie, Dr. Bud Burns, and Dr. T. J. McIllwaine were the teachers who left a great impression upon me. I also became close to Colonel H. P. Dunlop, headmaster of the academy. He recently died at about ninety-eight. The colonel and I kept in touch and usually talked about twice a year after I was elected to Congress. Many of our conversations focused on Social Security. I quelled his doubts and assured him that Congress was not going to let anything happen to Social Security.

Even though I was an average student at McCallie, the school curriculum prepared me for the next phase of my youth—college. In fact, when I went to Mississippi State, I had the jump on most incoming freshmen because I had already taken many of the same courses at McCallie and had the books. The three and a half years I spent at Mississippi State were enjoyable. Even before I was accepted to the school, there was no question in my mind that if I could obtain the funds I would go to Mississippi State College.

One of my main motivations for attending State had to do with my family ties to the school—the "Montgomery connection" that I mentioned earlier. My great-aunt Madge Montgomery, a writer and newspaperwoman, was one of my influential Montgomery ties. At one time in the early 1900s she owned what is now the *Meridian Star*. But it was my great-grandfather Colonel Montgomery who was probably the best-known Montgomery, not just in Starkville but throughout the entire state. Colonel Montgomery was a leader in Oktibbeha County. He owned the home the locals referred to as "the Cedars," which was located on the Starkville–West Point Road. He also owned more than ten thousand acres in Oktibbeha and the surrounding counties that he used primarily for farming, dairying, and raising Jersey cattle for sale (I think the family only owns about forty of these acres today). He also cultivated some row crops such as cotton. Colonel Montgomery was a graduate of Erskin College in South Carolina. He knew the value of education, and when he was elected to the Mississippi Legislature in the late 1890s he used his influence to assure the state's first A&M school would be in the town of Starkville.

In honor of his hard work and dedication to bring an A&M college to northeast Mississippi, the campus's Montgomery Hall was named in honor of the Colonel. Initially housing the agricultural school, the building has served many purposes. In 1996, the Mississippi legislature allocated $6 million to update the building. I worked very hard with the Mississippi legislature to see that funds for Montgomery Hall were in the larger bond bill. Senator Hob Bryan of Amory told me he would see that Montgomery Hall was added in the bond bill, and it was. Elevators are being added, and the artificial floors are being removed in order to return the building to its original splendor. When completed, you will be able to look from the ground floor all the way to the ceiling.

Unlike Stephen D. Lee, the school's first president, Colonel W. B. Montgomery did not fight for the Confederacy. Instead, he ran a successful ammunition plant in Montgomery, Alabama, for the Confederate forces. The "Colonel" was added to his name while he was running the plant. The name stuck, and he was referred to as Colonel until his death. And because of his hard work behind the scenes, work he had done to establish Mississippi A&M, I think the building named in his honor is a fitting tribute.

Family connections aside, I still had to work hard when I was at State. I enjoyed being a business major and made fairly good grades in college, but, as with anyone who has attended college, I feel I could have studied a bit more at times. But I was young and the world was opened up for me at State as I spent a great deal of time getting involved in student government. By my senior year I was elected president of the student body and named "Mr. Mississippi State." I made many close friends at State: Barney Boyles, Boo Ferris, Austin Ferrell, Jack Truitt, and Bill Murphy were just a few I remember.

I also participated in a variety of athletic activities, including varsity basketball. The coach of the team at the time, Dick Hitt, was an excellent teacher, and I enjoyed working with him. Although I was only a reserve player, I always tried to do my best. Track and field was another one of my athletic endeavors. I was a high jumper and cleared 5' 8" on several occasions. Our coach was William O. Spencer, who also taught in the Engineering School. State was still relatively small at the time, and many professors pulled double duty. I was also the manager of the football team my senior year. The three varsity coaches were Allyn McKeen, head coach; Murray Warmath, line coach; and Boyden Wyatt, end coach; and Dick Hitt, the freshman coach. The trainer, Dr. H. W. Wendler, who was an osteopath, later became the trainer for the Brooklyn Dodgers after World War II.

As you can probably tell, my roots in Mississippi run deep. Unfortunately, any landholdings that I once had in places like Oktibbeha County are now gone. After my father died, I inherited some of the family land in the county. Regretfully, I sold this land while I was at State in order to pay for college. I now know I should have held onto this land. I have frequently thought of buying some of the land that Colonel W. B. owned at one time. The family land in Starkville may be gone, but I am still proud to say that I left a successful business legacy in Mississippi. I lived with my mother and stepfather in Jackson after returning home from World War II until I could find something to do. (I detail my military service in chapter 2.) My first job was working for a sporting goods company, calling high school coaches and selling them football gear and basketball equipment. I traveled throughout the state in a very uncomfortable new Jeep.

But I survived, and after about a year on the job, I received a call from two of my friends at the Meyer and Rosenbaum Insurance Agency in Meridian, offering me a job as an agent for the firm. Al Rosenbaum and Lee Meyer, first cousins, owned the agency—one of the largest in east Mississippi. I weighed my options. I always thought I could sell insurance, especially fire and casualty so I accepted the job offer. Instead of selling fire and casualty insurance, however, I began my employment for Meyer and Rosenbaum selling life insurance for Aetna. My partner was Jimmie McLaurin, who was also associated with Meyer and Rosenbaum in their life insurance business. Unfortunately, my employment with Meyer and Rosenbaum did not last very long— about one year. I could never get the swing of selling life and health insurance.

Shortly after leaving Meyer and Rosenbaum I was offered a job by Sam T. Watts who ran Meridian Motors, a Ford dealership owned by Mr. DeWitt DeWeese of Philadelphia, Mississippi. I accepted the offer and began my career as a truck salesman. Initially, we were still not getting many trucks and cars because the economy was slowly shifting from war to peacetime commerce. Ford and other car companies were having to switch from making military equipment to producing automobiles. But the economic shift did not deter people from buying the merchandise that we had in stock. We had no problem selling every vehicle that came in. I made some good friends at the car dealership, including the Richardson brothers and the Mitchells, who worked in the service department.

My tenure as a car salesman only lasted about a year and a

half. I was getting restless to start my own business. I really wanted to get back into the insurance business, and I knew a little about fire and casualty policies based on my experience with Meyer and Rosenbaum. Determination and experience was not enough, though. I still needed a company to write insurance policies and a state insurance company–issued license. I would also need to take the exam in the commissioner's office. The state commissioner of the insurance department at the time was a capable insurance person named Walter Dell Davis.

I studied for the exam and passed it on the first try. I started my own agency in Meridian called the Montgomery Insurance Agency. The first step in owning my own business was complete. Since I'd returned from World War II, I'd always had in the back of mind that I wanted to be my own boss, and now the dream was becoming a reality.

The business grew quickly. I started with one company, but I was lucky. A Mr. Lippman from Atlanta heard I needed some other insurance companies to represent. Lippman represented General Insurance Company in Seattle, Washington, serving as their general agent. "The General," as it was referred to in the business, wrote all general lines, fire, casualty, and automobile full coverage insurance. The company also owned Safeco and all their automobile insurance lines of coverage. After I became affiliated with the General of Seattle, my coverage offerings increased because they offered an array of insurance for me to sell.

With my insurance offerings in place I opened my office in an old building off of Twenty-second Avenue. It was a walk-in office, but the building was showing its age and I soon moved to the more modern WMOX building. It was also at this time that I hired my first employee, Lorraine Fisher. Lorraine not only did her job well, she helped me organize the agency.

Initially, the business was not bringing in much revenue, but I had saved up enough money from my military earnings in World War II to carry the agency until it started turning a profit. The one and a half years it took the business to make money seemed like an eternity, but I was a pretty good agent and the business steadily grew. A large portion of this growth resulted from some of the friends I had made in the used car business. Whenever dealers sold a car and financed it through the bank, they needed insurance on the cars. Meridian car dealers like Marks Walker, Harold Walker, and Mac Couch referred the new owners to me. What made the deal even sweeter was that Meridian banks at that time were not insurance agents like they are now, and so we were able to write car insurance policies on bank loans.

After several years in the insurance business, I developed the idea of selling credit life insurance. The concept was that, for example, if someone bought a car and borrowed money from the bank for the purchase, the bank would write a life policy on the borrower. Should the borrower die, the loan would be paid off by the credit life insurance. Hence, the credit life insurance covered the loan owned by the bank. But for this plan to work, I needed a

Mississippi life insurance company to underwrite the credit life and let me serve as the general agent of these policies.

Throughout my life, I have been able to call upon my friends for support—emotional or financial. For the financial backing of my credit life insurance plan I turned to my friend J. Cliff Watts and his sister, Mrs. Kimbrell, who were the owners of the Greater Mississippi Life Insurance Company in Meridian. This company wrote burial insurance, and J. Cliff owned one of the two funeral homes in that part of the state. I approached J. Cliff and the chief of staff for Greater Mississippi Life, Charles Agnew, with my idea. They heard me out and said they liked the credit life insurance plan. With their blessing and monetary support I was licensed to sell their credit life insurance to Mississippi banks. We were now in business and soon developed comprehensive policies for the banks to sell to the consumer.

Again using my connections within the state, I began calling the few bankers I knew and immediately got them on board with the credit life insurance concept. The idea was a success from the start. This type of business was good for the banks and each bank that sold the insurance licensed a person in the bank to sell credit life. Moreover, this type of insurance did not compete with the regular insurers within the state. It was a moneymaker, and the banks, our insurance company, and I profited. This was the first time in my life that I can actually say that I made any real money.

As my business slowly but surely gained its financial footing we moved again. The Greater Mississippi Insurance Company bought the Threefoot building—a fifteen-story structure named after its original owners. Since I was now involved with the credit life division of Greater Mississippi, I moved my agency from the old WMOX building to the Greater Mississippi Life building. Fortunately, Greater Mississippi renamed the building after the company and eliminated any confusion about a fifteen-story "Threefoot" building in downtown Meridian.

Things were pretty stable when we moved into our new offices. I was now the general agent. Louise Sanders ran the processing and the general agency. Each month, different banks sent in the amount of money that came to the company and kept their percentage. As I said, these were stable times, and my business was doing well. Working in the insurance business was great. The agency did not tie me down, and I had the opportunity to get out and sell insurance throughout the state. And it was through my travels that I met many people, people that would eventually help me in my political career.

In 1955, I ran for the state senate when Senator Billy Gunn left the position after being appointed by Governor J. P. Coleman to be the fourteenth district's circuit judge. I ran against Lauderdale County school principal Donald Williamson. It was a close race, but I won by less than one hundred votes. My opponent ran a good campaign and won throughout the county, but it was the pro-Montgomery turnout in Meridian that got me over the top. I did not rest on my laurels following this election. After this race, I worked hard through the Meridian Chamber of Commerce–sponsored county meetings. This hard work proved beneficial as I easily won the next two elections.

My ten years in the Mississippi State Senate were busy ones. I worked on several pieces of legislation. For example, S.B. 2017 (1964) was an act "authorizing the Board of Supervisors of any county within the state to secure motor vehicle liability insurance, and for related purposes." Another bill that I authored was S.B. 1824 (1966), which "created an interagency commission on mental illness and retardation." These were among the more than one hundred bills and acts that I either authored or coauthored during my tenure in the Mississippi legislature.

Moreover, in the ten years that I served in the Mississippi senate, I never missed a vote—a record that still remains unchallenged.

I also served on committees during my days as state senator from Lauderdale County. I was vice chair of the Committee on Aviation (1957) and member of the Committee on the Inauguration of the Governor (1964), and I ran for president pro tempore of the state senate (1964) but was beaten by Senator George Yarbrough of Red Banks.

I enjoyed the work on these committees because it enabled me to make connections with other folks throughout the state. Lieutenant Governor Carrol Gartin was among those people.

Gartin was elected lieutenant governor in 1964. Not only was he great to work with, but I also enjoyed visiting with his wife and two children very much.

I also enjoyed working with United States Senator John C. Stennis. As a state senator, I worked with Senator Stennis's office on many federal and state projects. This working relationship eventually developed into a very close friendship. The senator and I believed in and worked for the people of Mississippi. Plus, we were both proud State alumni; I was proud of Senator Stennis as our highest government officer who graduated from Mississippi State. When the Senator came to Jackson or Meridian he always let me know where he was, and I considered myself his lieutenant in Mississippi.

I enjoyed my time in the Mississippi state senate because I could work for my company and in government. But after ten years in the Mississippi legislature, I wanted to move on to another political position. I wanted to take on another challenge, and I thought about running for lieutenant governor when the next election arrived. This was not the first time I had thought about seeking the state's second-highest office. Back in the early 1950s I toyed with the idea, but before I announced my candidacy I was called up with the 31st Infantry "Dixie" Division to serve in the Korean War. So there went my idea of running for lieutenant governor. I served two years in the Korean War and came back to Meridian after the war.

The idea of running for lieutenant governor in 1966 soon gave way to another political aspiration when the opportunity to run for the United States Congress presented itself. Congressman Prentiss Walker from Smith County had been in the United States House of Representatives for two years, having beaten incumbent Arthur Winstead. Winstead had served as our congressman for twenty-two years, and he thought Prentiss, a Republican, did not present a threat to his reelection. Never underestimate the opposition.

Prentiss served two years in the House and then decided he wanted to be a U.S. Senator. He ran for the Senate in 1966 against Senator Jim Eastland and was defeated. Prentiss's defeat meant opportunity for me because the U.S. Congress seat in my district was now open.

I had to make a big decision regarding a run for my district's congressional seat. After all, if I won, I would be away from home and my prospering insurance business. So I began to ask for advice on the matter. One of the people I turned to was Senator Stennis, a seasoned politician who knew the ins and outs of Washington politics. The senator discussed the issue with me, neither encouraging nor discouraging my bid for the congressional seat. Stennis knew that the choice was mine and mine alone to make, and after much thought and the support of my friends I decided to run for Congress.

The primaries came and went, and I was elected, out of four other contenders, as the Democratic candidate for my district. Out of this group, J. O. Hollis of Carthage was probably my toughest opponent. I worked hard to win this primary. It was a close vote, and we were not even sure I had won at first. John McLaurin of Brandon and Ben Hilbun of Starkville represented me on the election board. After the votes were carefully counted we finally came out with one hundred more votes than my opponents.

The winner coming out of the Republican primary was my friend and golfing buddy, Mac McAllister from Meridian. We had a spirited race despite the fact that there were twice as many Democrats as Republicans in the district. It was a close election, but I prevailed and was elected to the U.S. Congress in 1966, with my first term beginning the following January.

When I arrived in Washington in January 1967, Senator Stennis and his office were most helpful. Eph Creswell from Durant ran the senator's office in Washington and was kind to my campaign manager, Bob Montgomery of Canton, who had come with me to run my Washington office. Bob stayed two years with me and then went on to serve in the Mississippi legislature. Mildred Ward and others in Senator Stennis's office were very helpful to my staff as well. Also lending a hand was Senator Eastland's staff, but we were closer to Senator Stennis and his personnel.

In the meantime, I thought I could run both of my businesses and serve in Washington at the same time. I soon realized you cannot run a business and serve in Washington. Some of my fellow congressmen faced a similar predicament. They had law practices and businesses back home and realized they had neither the time nor the energy to do both. I realized that if I focused on one obligation the other would suffer. I just could not keep up at the Mississippi office, and it was not fair to my customers, the agency, or my banking friends. So, after about two years in office I sold the agency to Mrs. Mary Aycock, and I resigned as general agent for my credit life connection. Bob Wright, a retired naval aviator, took over my position with Greater Mississippi. With my business issues settled by 1969, I could now turn my attention to my political career, a career that would span three decades.

Certainly, there were the typical hardships and disappointments during my early years. But I managed to survive and become stronger as a result of the adversities I experienced. And while I now spend the majority of my time in the Washington, D.C., area, it is my Mississippi roots that keep me grounded and humble. I still have my home in Meridian and go there about once a month.

II

Military Service

I have always liked the military, and, as a youth in Meridian, I longed to be a member of the armed forces and wear a uniform. In the early 1930s, I noticed people in the National Guard and how they wore their Army or Air Force uniforms on Monday nights, the night designated for National Guard drills. It was not until after the Korean and Vietnam wars that the National Guard and Reserves began drilling just on weekends on a monthly basis. Having participated in both the Monday and weekend drills, I prefer the latter because you have more time to learn about your job.

My military career began early in life. While some family customs may be a burden to those who remain to carry them out, the tradition of military participation in my family proved no such problem. My great-aunt in Starkville wanted me to attend the military high school that her son had attended—McCallie School in Chattanooga, Tennessee. McCallie is a college preparatory school for boys located on Missionary Ridge near Chattanooga. The McCallie brothers, Spencer Jarnagin and James Park McCallie, with the support of their father, the Rev. T. H. McCallie, founded the academy in 1905. I went to this fine institution in 1937 and wore the blue uniform. I was so proud of that uniform that during semester breaks at home I always wore my McCallie blues at Christmas and Easter dinners. On several occasions, people commented that they liked me in uniform—a well-received compliment since I was already fond of military attire.

McCallie offered a structured program that prepared its students for college and life by promoting academic, physical, spiritual, and emotional growth. The daily close order drill and battalion parades nurtured our physical and emotional development. Largely because of my previous drill experience with the Boy Scouts, these particular exercises came easy. Although we were all classified as Junior ROTC we received no class credit for participating in these courses. But I was inspired by this experience and had made up my mind that if I went to Mississippi State College (now Mississippi State University) I was going to stay in the ROTC for the whole four years and earn an officer's commission for my efforts.

I attended Mississippi State in the fall of 1939 and, like all freshmen males, took the mandatory two years of ROTC—a requirement I was more than happy to fulfill. The leader of my company, Company "F," was Captain M. E. Branigin, a fair man. Based on my experiences with the Boy Scouts and at McCallie, I knew I would enjoy the ROTC classes and the drills—and I did.

After two years of compulsory service in the ROTC, one could volunteer for another two-year stint if he was so inclined. This

voluntary service, plus surviving a senior year of military summer camp, meant a possible promotion to second lieutenant in
Army infantry, artillery, engineer, or supply units upon graduation. I do not believe there was any type of air ROTC (called
AFROTC today) at Mississippi State at the time. This branch of
the military fell under the Army and was classified as the "air
corps" during World War II.

As Mississippi State's yearbook, the *Reveille*, stated, I had
"caught the spirit of the times" as I along with my fellow cadets
strove to "better fit [ourselves] to serve in the Army of the United
States." So, in the fall of 1943 I applied to the advanced ROTC,
was accepted, and served as "Major, S-3, Plans and Training Officer" for my regiment. Meanwhile, the United States' full-scale
involvement in World War II began in December 1941. Any
American male between the ages of eighteen and twenty-five
who was physically and mentally able to march off to war did not
have long to wait. The same situation applied to my fellow cadets
at Mississippi State and me; soon we would be called out of college to go to war. During the month of January 1943, senior
ROTC program participants, myself included, were sent to Officers Candidate School (OCS). We missed May graduation exercises. In fact, it was not until May 2001 that I actually received
my formal diploma from Mississippi State University.

On January 16, 1943, I received the paperwork that sent me to
Fort Knox, Kentucky, for four months of OCS training for my
commission. I arrived in Fort Knox on February 14, via Camp

Shelby, Mississippi, for "the purpose of attending Officer Candidate School" and was assigned to class "No. 34." What followed was four months of intensive training. We drilled, had classes, learned about the current war, and experienced tough mental and physical training in preparation for the rigors of battlefield leadership. Throughout the month of January we trained outside in the cold. Fortunately, we received a reprieve from the elements, as our barracks were quite comfortable.

After a few months, my training at Fort Knox concluded. I had made it through officers training and got my second lieutenant bars in armor in May of 1943. Evidently, my previous military preparation had readied me for the rigors of officer training. Out of the 150 in our class about 30 candidates dropped out or failed the final qualifying exams. Those who survived the ordeal had a ceremony at Fort Knox, and I, along with my fellow officers, had our lieutenant bars pinned on us in front of family and friends. But the euphoria from this event was short-lived. I was soon called to active duty.

Prior to departure for Europe, I had a three-week leave in Mississippi. I enjoyed my brief stay, and I got to wear my snazzy Army uniform the entire time. Finally, my orders came, and I was sent to Camp Barkley, Texas, where I was assigned to a motorcycle platoon. I got to ride a Harley Davidson and served as commander of this reconnaissance platoon. There was one little snag in this assignment—I did not know how to ride a motorcycle. This obstacle did not deter me, however, as I quickly learned how to ride the Harley. Ironically, after I had learned how to ride the motorcycle and led the reconnaissance platoon for three months, the Army eliminated the motorcycle reconnaissance unit, and I was out of a job. In Europe motorcycles were everywhere during the war. The British and French used motorcycles more than Jeeps.

Despite the disappointment I had experienced with the motorcycle reconnaissance platoon, all was not lost. While stationed at Camp Barkley I had met some other officers in the division. These gentlemen had heard that the division commander Major General Carlos Brewer needed an aide-de-camp. I was then recommended for the job by some of these fellows. I got the position as aide-de-camp and thoroughly enjoyed my work, but, alas, this job, like motorcycle reconnaissance, would not last for very long. While on maneuvers in Texas, my division performed poorly, thus relieving General Brewer of his duties. I was again without a job.

After a short stint of unemployment, I was assigned to the Combat Command A (CCA) of the Twelfth Armored Division and we were promptly sent to Europe. When we arrived in England we sat and waited for the whole division, which included tanks, equipment, and personnel, to make the trip across the Atlantic.

On or around December 9, 1944, the supplies and men arrived, and our command unit was formed. Brigadier General Riley Ennis joined our division in England and was eventually made commander of CCA, my unit. Combat Command unit A quickly became two fighting forces, Combat Commands A & B. These commands of tank battalions, infantry battalions, artillery battalions, engineering reconnaissance, supply and other support units comprised this complicated organization. General Ennis had to maneuver men and machines while taking care to accomplish the mission as it was relayed from the higher-ups. I did not envy his position.

I was General Ennis's aide and assisted him as he ran Combat A. I gave no real orders to the troops nor did I lead a battalion. Instead, I served as a liaison between General Ennis and CCA. This job basically entailed me shuffling between combat commands to deliver messages and observe the movements and locations of our infantry and tank battalions. I had to pay special attention to the details of our actions to ensure that I did not overshoot our forces and engage the Germans or cause us to become prisoners of war. It was our goal, since we were an armored division, to break out of the front lines and race down the autobahn and get behind the German lines to force their surrender. More important, I often carried sensitive information with me that, if seized by the enemy, could have wrought disastrous consequences to my command units.

Eventually I established a routine: once in my Jeep in either France or Germany I traveled between one armored headquarters and another. This practice remained fairly consistent, and I got to know some of the back roads within the perimeter of my command unit—or so I thought. One day I was going to Command Unit B. Apparently, I got ahead of all our forces and ended up in enemy territory. As I came over a hill I heard some shouting off in the distance ordering me to stop my Jeep. I soon discovered that the people yelling at me were American reconnaissance forces. Evidently, my command was actually ahead of our advancing American forces. I immediately identified myself and met some of the members of the unit in the road. One of the men asked if I had seen the enemy. Producing the map of where I had just traveled, I showed them my route and told them that I had not seen the enemy. The unit's commander scanned the map and thanked me as he ordered his troops to move onto the next intersection as I had just been in that area of no man's land.

Another war adventure involved the capturing of a German machine-gun emplacement at Ludwigshafen, Germany. On March 23, 1945, I was advancing with the infantry on the outskirts of this southwestern German town on the Rhine River when I saw the machine-gun emplacement. As the report said, I "personally [helped] capture an enemy machinegun emplacement that had been inflicting casualties among the units to which [I] was attached." For this deed I was awarded the Bronze Star Medal for Valor. But what made me the proudest was that we had the Germans on the run. The war was over in June of that same year.

As the war wound down in Europe, we discovered some of the German POW camps where they held Allied and Jewish prisoners of war. Just prior to the conflict's end, my command unit descended the autobahn, and we began seeing Allied prisoners. Evidently, the German guards heard we were on the march and fled the camps to avoid capture, and their prisoners escaped unmolested.

I saw hundreds of half-starved Jewish captives wandering along the road. Seeing their despair, I directed them down the road, where they found Allied support units to feed and clothe them. I saw more British prisoners than Americans. The sight of all the prisoners saddened me. The Germans had mistreated all of their captives—all of the Allied inmates were in poor health and hungry. I was, in some cases, the first American these prisoners had seen since their capture.

As I passed Hitler's victims on the road and gave them directions to the support units, I did so with extreme confidence. I knew the Germans had fled. But some of the enemy did appear as we marched down the road. On several occasions some came out of hiding from the woods and homes in the surrounding areas and surrendered. Defeated and dejected, these stragglers of the once mighty German war machine were helpless. So helpless, in fact, that I did not attempt to take their weapons. Instead, I directed them down the road where they were captured and placed in a prisoner-of-war facility.

The war ended, and my unit, as well as other units by this time, had all of these German prisoners. Only the German SS troops were retained; the others were sent home. The SS troops were Hitler's elite fighting force and their atrocities against humanity have been well documented. Once they were rounded up, the SS prisoners were placed in one of the several temporary prisoner-of-war camps distributed throughout the country. I was put in charge of one of these camps, which had about two thousand prisoners out in a field. Unfortunately, a rumor started that the Allies would systematically kill these prisoners, prompting several suicides amongst the captives. The Allies tried very few Germans for war crimes, and the ones that were tried were the Nazi leaders, not the common SS soldiers. After about a week the camp disbanded, and most of the prisoners were sent home.

My time in Europe had been adventurous. I traveled throughout the continent, served as a liaison between command posts, and won the Bronze Star for Valor, a European Theater Ribbon with three combat stars, and the Magnolia Award. But none of these experiences or accolades secured a job. My commander, General Ennis, got his orders to return to the States, and I was left in Europe without an assignment. I did not, however, drift for long; in late July of 1945 orders sending me to the Pacific Theater arrived. With the bombings of Hiroshima and Nagasaki and the subsequent treaty with Japan in August of 1945, the war in Japan was over. I stayed in Europe for another year as aide to General Roderick Allen, who was personnel commander in Frankfurt, Germany. One of the perks of the job was that I had my own car. Sometimes I drove a Packard Clipper I 20 five-passenger sedan or checked out a Maybach sedan.

Evidently, General Allen appreciated my services, and on February 12, 1946, I was awarded the Army Commendation Ribbon. In his letter regarding the honor, Allen said, "your exceptionally meritorious service as my Aide de Camp during the period July 1945 to February 1946, warrant special mention and commendation upon my departure from the 1st Armored Division." He continued, "your enthusiasm, energy and loyalty together with your good judgment and capacity for making friends relieved me of many time-consuming tasks. Your services reflect great credit on yourself on the highest traditions of the United States Army." These were very kind words from a good friend.

General Allen went to the Korean War for another tour of duty for his country. Another aide, named Frank R. Pagnotta, went with General Allen to Korea. World War II was over, and I, now Captain Montgomery, headed for home. But my military career was far from over; I was about to join the Mississippi National Guard.

At more than three hundred years old, the National Guard of the United States is really older than the nation itself. The Guard's origins can be traced back to the earliest English colonies in what is now the United States. Prior to their independence from England, colonists formed their own militia or "National Guard" to protect their individual towns and villages. These colonial militias fended off Indian attacks and foreign invaders and later helped lead the fledgling nation to victory in the Revolutionary War.

Once nationhood was established, the Guard organized as a national military and community support unit. The National Guard today has two missions: support our nation in time of war, and support the governor of the state in case of a natural disaster or civilian disturbance. The National Guard serves its state with the governor in command authorized to use the Guard as he or she sees fit. The governor's power can be usurped only by the president, who by law can order the Guard from the different states to a particular crisis. For its part, the federal government pays the drill salaries of each officer and enlisted person and furnishes all the equipment, weapons, tanks, and airplanes.

Because of its service tradition, I have always been partial to the National Guard, especially the Mississippi National Guard. This adoration goes back as far as my primary, junior high, and high school days. As you will recall, the Monday nights the National Guard wore their uniforms around town are favorite memories of mine. And, like any young boy, I enjoyed the big trucks the local guard units had. Above all, I admired the men and the officers who were in the National Guard in my home-town—the role models an impressionable lad admired while growing up.

It was with a sense of joy and commitment that I became a member of the Guard after my return from World War II. At this time there was a particular need for Guardsmen because all the Mississippi units had been called to war. The Air Guard units in

Meridian, Jackson, and Gulfport were among the many units called to active duty. Their planes, however, were outdated and not sent overseas.

I was a captain when I returned from World War II but accepted a reduction to first lieutenant to serve in the Meridian tank unit. I wanted to serve in Company A, 198th Tank Battalion of the Mississippi National Guard, so I along with my old friend, Billy Mitts, accepted our demotions.

Captain Wallace Heitman led the company. We had a full unit of 100 officers and men; there were no vacancies. The lack of space in the 198th Battalion inspired me to form another tank company in Meridian. I took this idea to the new adjutant general, Pat Wilson, a wounded World War II veteran, and fellow Mississippi State alum. I told Wilson that I had been in an armored tank division during the war and wanted to create another M4A3 tank unit in Meridian. My war experiences, I further explained, included working with M4A3 tanks. In other words, I did know something about tanks and tank warfare. General Wilson agreed and granted me permission to create the new tank company.

As I set about constructing the new tank company, I appointed my friends Billie Curtis and Wayne Wahrendoff to the two full-time positions within the unit. Both men entered the unit as sergeants, and over the years they reached officer status. Over a span of fifteen years Curtis became a full colonel and Wahredoff rose to chief warrant officer.

My company was staffed, and the roster quickly filled. We drilled at Key Field in an old Air Guard Hanger. This armory was ideal for my unit because the facility afforded us a place to drill and recruit. The recruiting process was easy because some men had been in World War II and, like me, wanted to continue to serve their country. Other recruits had been too young for combat during World War II and wanted now to enlist in the National Guard.

The National Guard's appeal was wide-ranging. Members served their nation and were paid well for making Monday night drills. Eventually, they served on the weekends and at a summer camp, thus giving the young men and women who participated in these maneuvers a second income. Also, there is a great retirement program for guardsmen and reservists who serve for twenty years or more that can be drawn after age sixty.

Obviously, I see the program as essential to the nation's security, but there is a dangerous side to this obligation. Small firefights constantly erupt throughout the world, and there is always a chance a Guard or Reserve unit will be called up. During World War II and the wars in Korea and Vietnam, the odds of units being called into active duty increased. There is also the chance that a governor might call up units to assist in state disasters such as floods and riots. By serving in the Guard or Reserves, members run the risk of being taken away from their daily lives to tend to large-scale emergencies.

I have been called upon to serve abroad and at home while in the Guard. First, my National Guard Tank Company was called up during the Korean War. After World War II the attempts to reunify Korea failed. In 1948 the North established the (communist) People's Republic of Korea while the South announced it was the (democratic) Republic of Korea. A line was drawn between the two, the Forty-eighth Parallel. By June 1950, the Communist-backed North Koreans crossed over into the South and war broke out. The United Nations defended South Korea, and, as a result, the United States, along with Britain, Canada, Australia, and Turkey joined in the fray. By October 1950, Communist China sided with North Korea. As outlined in the Truman Doctrine, it was the United States' obligation to help any and all nations fighting against Communism. This meant that U.S. troops would be sent over to Korea to assist in the UN peacekeeping efforts.

In December of 1950 my Guard unit left on a troop train from Meridian and was gone for two years. The unit was blended with the Thirty-first Infantry "Dixie" Division comprised of units from all parts of Mississippi and Alabama, and we ended up in Fort Jackson, South Carolina. Fortunately, or unfortunately, depending on your perspective about such things, my unit never saw any overseas duty during the Korean War. Although some officers and men from my unit were sent to Korea at certain times, our unit as a whole never saw any action there. I was one of the officers from my unit who was called to go overseas to the war area, but the war, which essentially ended in a stalemate in

1953, was winding down before I arrived in late 1951. The only real proof I have that I was involved with the Korean War is a letter from Major General A. G. Paxton, USA Commanding Officer, to Lieutenant General Doyle Hickey, Far East Commander. In this letter, Paxton described my service in Korea, telling Hickey that my "shipping out of the Division [was] over [his] personal objection" and that he had made every effort to retain me. He also said, "Sonny has a marvelous personality, possesses a special knack of doing the right thing at the right time, gets along with both superiors and subordinates, and always gets the job done." I am particularly pleased with this statement because I have always dealt with people on a fair and personable level. These comments by Major General Paxton are as appreciated now as they were fifty years ago.

When I returned to Mississippi, after a little over a year, my orders were changed, and the Thirty-first Division was deactivated about six months after the Korean War's conclusion. I have no real war stories to tell from this adventure. No captured machine-gun emplacements or running a POW camp this go-around. But working with my fellow guardsmen and under the command of men such as Major General A. G. Paxton during the Korean War was a valuable experience.

Upon my Meridian homecoming I heard of an opening of a major's slot in a transportation battalion, and I applied for and filled the position. For several years I served in this capacity under the command of Lieutenant Colonel Tom Minniece, a prominent lawyer in my hometown. Minniece eventually moved to state headquarters in Jackson and was promoted to full colonel. Minniece departed, and I was promoted to lieutenant colonel and served as commander of this battalion. My command was responsible for the large trucks and semis with trailers. I am sure you have seen the convoys of these vehicles at some time or another while traveling America's highways.

Sometimes duty calls overseas in far-off locations such as Korea, while other situations call for service at home. During the civil rights movement my unit was called upon to maintain the peace. The late 1950s and 1960s were tumultuous times for the Deep South and Mississippi in particular as we adjusted to the new integration laws as set forth by the federal government. While the majority of southerners accepted these changes, some reacted violently to the integration of schools, bus stations, and other public facilities.

In May of 1965 my unit escorted the Freedom Riders across the state. Initially, this interracial civil rights group, organized by James Farmer, national director of the Congress of Racial Equality (CORE), was testing the court order *Boyton v. Virginia* (1960). This mandate stated that any and all segregation in railways and bus terminals was illegal. In May of 1961 the riders made their first trips through Georgia, Alabama, and Mississippi and were greeted with violence in places like Anniston, Alabama, where a bus was burned and riders were attacked. But the Freedom Riders pressed on, and by November 1961, the Interstate Commerce Commission finally stepped in and prohibited the segregation of public accommodations. But the federal mandate did not stop the violence, and it was for this reason that my unit was called in to protect these riders in 1965.

Integration-related violence had occurred in the state in the past, as with the 1962 integration of the University of Mississippi by James Meredith and Freedom Summer of 1964. So, as you can well imagine, each time a protest or testing of a new civil rights law occurred in Mississippi, the knowledge of past violence created a tense situation.

At the time I was a lieutenant colonel of the transportation battalion out of Meridian. A phone call from the adjutant general of Mississippi instructed me to take some of the men in my battalion to ensure the safe passage of the civil rights activists. My orders were fairly simple: meet the two Freedom Rider buses traveling from Montgomery, Alabama, to the west coast and escort them through Mississippi. Our orders also included bringing our weapons for protection (.45-caliber pistols or the M-1 carbine rifle). I took my men and met the buses at the Mississippi-Alabama state line and relieved the Alabama Guardsmen who had escorted the group through the Heart of Dixie. The Freedom Rider buses arrived with the Alabama Highway Patrol leading them, the Alabama Guardsmen, including their adjutant general, General Graham, onboard, and Guard trucks loaded with troops right behind. After the Alabama Guardsmen exited the two buses I decided that I would supervise the lead bus and put Captain Giles Patty in charge of the second bus.

Accompanied by Sergeant Billie Curtis, a few of my armed National Guardsmen and I boarded the first bus. My intent, as well as my troops', was to protect the passengers on the bus. We were armed because we did not know who might attack the buses as they traveled through Mississippi. Moreover, per my instructions, some of the weapons were not even loaded.

When I got on the bus with my troops, I welcomed the Freedom Riders to Mississippi and assured their safe passage through the state. Some members of the national press were on the bus, and they noted my greeting in their newspaper columns.

More interesting than what the newspapers had to say were a couple of the passengers on my bus that day. John Lewis and Bob Filner were the two people that I remember. Lewis was a prominent leader of the civil rights movement. He was a supporter of Dr. Martin Luther King Jr., played a very important role in the organization of the Student Nonviolent Community Committee (SNCC), which he chaired from 1963 to 1966, and participated in the March on Washington in 1963. At the time of our initial encounter, Lewis was in his twenties and I was in my thirties. Ironically, we both ended up serving in the United States Congress. I, of course, served Mississippi and began my work in 1967. Lewis continues to serve the state of Georgia. He began his congressional service in 1986, representing the state's Fifth District.

When he was a freshman representative I approached Lewis and reminded him of the day he rode on my bus during the Mississippi Freedom Rides of 1965. We reminisced about that fateful day and eventually became close friends and still see each other occasionally.

Also on my bus that day was a nineteen-year-old Ivy-leaguer named Bob Filner. In 1992, Filner was elected to represent California's Fiftieth District in Congress. As it turned out, Filner ended up serving on my Veterans' Committee, and we also became good friends. I see him often even though I have left Congress. When we first met in the halls of Capitol Hill, Filner informed me that after he, Lewis, and the other riders exited the bus in Jackson, they were arrested and put in jail. Several days later they were moved to Parchman Penitentiary in the Mississippi Delta. Here, they were held for three weeks before they were released. But the incarceration of these Freedom Riders was something that was out of my control.

I felt that my Guard unit did its job. As the bus traveled through Mississippi, the Freedom Riders and the members of the press wanted me to stop the bus so they could relieve themselves. This bus had no toilet facilities, and it had been more than four hours since they had left Montgomery, Alabama. I should have stopped the bus and let them relieve themselves like Captain Patty did with the second bus group. In hindsight, Captain Patty's judgment was better than mine because my passengers could never settle down because of their discomfort.

The only real moment of tension on this ride, for me personally, was when we went through my hometown of Meridian. The Trailways bus we were riding on stopped at all of its regular stations, including Meridian. While at the Meridian stop, some hotheads spotted me on the bus and shouted at me for protecting the Freedom Riders. It was funny, however, that these Meridian-to-Jackson ticket holders saw we were armed and never boarded the bus. They sheepishly said they would catch the next bus. Just outside of Newton on Highway 80, the bus, as was customary, stopped for anyone who waved it down. An elderly woman hailed the bus. We opened the door, and the woman saw all the guns and people wearing steel helmets and said, "Lordy, I don't believe I want to ride on the bus. I will go to Jackson tomorrow."

We continued down the road escorted by Mississippi Highway Patrol. Our rate of speed was eighty miles per hour, and I told the bus driver to slow it down a bit because I did not want to crash. It took us about an hour and a half to make it from Meridian to Jackson—a fast trip considering it normally took about two hours to make this same trek back then. When we pulled into the Jackson bus station, I let the Freedom Riders and the press off the bus. All the passengers rushed to the restrooms and were immediately arrested and jailed.

Relieved of our Freedom Rider escort duties my unit filed an "after action" report at the Jackson National Guard Armory. While we were filing the report and returning our weapons in the parking lot at the Jackson Armory, several full-time guardsmen, who were in the Military Police Unit and rode in the convoy, approached us. While conversing about the day's events with these gentlemen I noticed they were armed with riot-type shotguns. Well, as the MPs unloaded these weapons from their trucks I guess one of them accidentally dropped his shotgun and it discharged. The buckshot went up in the air and luckily none of us were harmed.

The accidental firearm discharge at the Jackson Armory was the only shot fired during this Freedom Riders' episode. We had brought the Freedom Riders through the Magnolia State safely and without incident. I was proud of this accomplishment as well as the other times the National Guard of Mississippi served its citizens during hurricanes and other emergencies—natural or man-made.

Following the Freedom Rides, I served as commander of my unit for about four years. It was during my fourth year in this capacity that I was moved to state headquarters in Jackson and promoted to full colonel. By 1966 I was involved with the Guard, ran a business, and was elected to the United States Congress. With the election over, I found myself, as it should have been, spending more and more time in Washington, D.C., tending to my duties as a Mississippi representative. Nonetheless, I still made my drills on the weekends. Instead of flying all the way to Meridian, however, I served with the Washington, D.C., National Guard at the D.C. Armory across the street from the Kennedy Stadium, where the Washington Redskins used to play. The experiences with the D.C. Guard were pleasurable. I enjoyed drilling with this unit and made several friends from the D.C. area. When the D.C. Guard was called to disturbances in Washington, however, I was merely an observer rather than an active participant.

In the late 1960s I was promoted to brigadier general in the Mississippi Army National Guard and assistant chief of the Mississippi National Guard. Major General Beebe Turnage, adjutant general, had endorsed me because Major General Shield Simms of Columbus had retired from the post earlier in the year.

Before I could receive my new stars, I had to attend Command and General Staff School in Fort Leavenworth, Kansas. Enrolling in the program was not difficult, but being able to attend classes and still serve in Congress proved to be a tricky proposition. I was permitted to miss some days in Congress to fulfill my obligations in Fort Leavenworth, but I logged many air miles shuttling back and forth between General Staff School and Washington, D.C. Also, because I was in Congress, my time at the school was spent more as lecturer than a student. But I learned about war tactics, graduated, and was promoted to brigadier general.

There was a service for this promotion at the Governor's Mansion in Jackson. The governor at the time, Bill Waller, pinned on one star, and my mother pinned on the other. It was a very enjoyable occasion for me and my family and friends in attendance.

The promotion to brigadier general was really a big step in my life and has meant so much to me. The people of Mississippi and in Washington often call me "General" because of my National Guard title and military record. I now hold the title of major general, given to me when I retired from the Guard. I almost did not achieve this rank because, in the early 1970s, the Defense Department decided that members of Congress could not serve in both Congress and the Guard simultaneously, forcing many of my fellow statesmen to become inactive. Fortunately for me, the governor served as my commander and only he could rule me inactive. So I remained active and rose through the ranks to my current status. In March 1970 I was honored as one of the two members of the Congress still active in the Guard. Today, the ruling has changed and congressmen do not have to go inactive because of their congressional obligations.

As you can probably discern by now, the National Guard has held extreme significance throughout my life. I do not know of any organization, other than church, that has meant more to me than the Guard. I knew that my service in the National Guard, and to the same extent, my service in the Army during World War II, was helping my community, state, and nation. Moreover, by assisting my local population I was aiding the folks in my community whom I had grown up with.

The camaraderie within the unit itself is also very important to me. The love for each other within our Guard unit was unbelievable. When families of fellow guardsmen were in peril, everyone in the unit pitched in and tried to help. This is the point that

I try to emphasize when I discuss the Guard: we help each other out when needed. The National Guard has been like a parent to me, and when I have needed help it has and will always be there.

The leadership within the Mississippi Guard was incredible as well. All adjutant generals in the state that I served under were excellent leaders. Major General Pat Wilson was my first adjutant general, and he served for sixteen years—longer than any other Mississippi adjutant general ever served. Only the adjutant general of South Carolina, who served thirty years, served longer than Wilson. Moreover, General Wilson was a kind person. As I recall, every interaction with Pat Wilson and his lovely wife, Ms. Annie, was pleasant.

Walter Johnson followed Wilson. Like Wilson, Johnson was an excellent leader and proved to be a superior adjutant general for the state's National Guard. Walter was also a World War II hero who flew fighter aircraft and was shot down over Germany, bailed out, and was a prisoner of war. Johnson left and was followed by Beebe Turnage, a state district judge from Monticello, Mississippi. Turnage, like his predecessors, displayed excellent leadership qualities. Beebe promoted me to brigadier general in the Guard.

The value of serving in the National Guard cannot be overstated. So, when I served in Congress I did all I could to assist the National Guard and Reserves. My friends at the National Guard Bureau, which included Major General Fran Greenlief, Lieutenant General John Conaway, and Lieutenant General Ed Baca, were vital in helping pass important legislation related to the National Guard. Generals Baca and Conaway were especially helpful. General Conaway has become a very close friend, and we have established business connections together. Whenever I have asked for his help, he has always been there. General Baca was also very helpful, especially when he served as chief of the National Guard Bureau. Baca even named an award in my honor that is given to an outstanding guardsman each year. Even though he has moved back to New Mexico, he and his wife have remained good friends, and I see him when he comes to Washington as a consultant. General Conaway and I have breakfast together in Washington at least three times a week.

While in the House of Representatives, I did everything I could to preserve and strengthen the United States National Guard Reserve. Throughout my years in the House I corresponded with presidents, sent out memorandums, and spoke before the House Armed Services Committee and on the House floor regarding the protection and maintenance of the National Guard's funding and programs. In a letter I wrote to Jimmy Carter just before he took office I told the newly elected commander-in-chief that I was "a strong advocate for the National Guard and Reserves." In 1974, I sponsored and was instrumental in the passage of several bills that benefited the National Guard and Reserves. One of these bills, passed during the Ninety-fourth Congress, authorized tuition assistance and reenlistment bonuses for enlisted members and officers of the National Guard and Reserves—an idea that I incorporated in the new GI Bill. The list of bills related to the National Guard presented, waiting in committee, amended, and so forth that I worked on during my terms in office would fill an entire book. As I wrote in a letter to my fellow colleagues on the Armed Services Committee in January of 1977, "During our Armed Services Committee Meetings, I have been known to expound on the capabilities and successes of the National Guard and Reserve forces." How true these words were and still are today.

Even though I am retired from the National Guard and Congress, I along with other retirees from the Guard have taken an active role in preserving this American institution. We all continue to expound on the importance of the Guard. The National Guard Association of the United States (NGAUS) with Major General Retired Dick Alexander, the executive director, really fights for the National Guard in Congress. The association, comprised of Air Guard and Army officers, is constantly working with the Authorization and Appropriations Committees in both the House and the Senate. Also, the association devotes a majority of its time to working with the Guard units in every state.

The National Guard Association of the United States, comprised of officers and retired officers in the National Guard, does a great service to the officer corps of the National Guard. It is a strong organization that works with Congress to see that affairs of the Guard are treated fairly. Every year NGAUS has one of the largest National Guard–related conferences, and every year the president of the United States comes to the meeting to speak.

The Enlisted Association of the National Guard of the United States (EANGUS) is another National Guard advocate. EANGUS has twice as many members in their association as NGAUS because there are more sergeants than officers in the Guard. The chief executive officer is Sgt. Mike Cline, who does an outstanding job. NGAUS and EANGUS work closely together in Washington. I am proud to be associated with both groups, especially since I, along with Sergeant Virgil Williams of Gulfport, organized the Mississippi Non Commissioned Officers Association (NCO), which later became EANGUS. Each year the NCO participates in the EANGUS conference and is also working with other states to form their own national organizations. EANGUS awards the G. V. "Sonny" Montgomery Award to the congressional staff member who has helped the National Guard the most in a given year.

My years in the Army and the National Guard were very rewarding physically, intellectually, and spiritually. My progress, be it from ROTC lieutenant to Army captain or National Guard lieutenant to major general, was valuable and helped me face life's challenges. I especially appreciate the leadership skills and the lifelong friendships I have made through my military experiences. They have served me well in both my political and personal life.

III

Presidents with Whom
I Have Served

L yndon Johnson had two years left of his presidency when I got to Washington in 1967. I went to the White House along with thirteen freshman Democrats to meet with the president. We got there at 6 P.M., and the President talked till 9 P.M. We got no water or food during the entire time.

At about 8 P.M., one freshman, Bill Nichols of Alabama, got up and told the president that his wife was waiting on him. I wanted to leave too but I would never get up on a president to leave until given permission by him.

I liked President Johnson but never got to know him very well. With the mounting pressures on and criticisms of him because of the Vietnam War, he decided not to seek reelection.

I remember he made a point of having a person stand behind him in the receiving line whether at the White House or in one of his visits to the Congress. This person would tell the president each individual's first name so that he could use it when he shook hands with him or her.

He really knew the workings of Congress, having been the leader of the U.S. Senate. He kept the Democratic leadership of the House on their toes, and he got through most of the legislation he wanted. Right before I came to Washington, he got his welfare and "helping the poor" legislation through Congress.

He had strange working hours. He would sleep a couple of hours in the afternoon and work until eleven or twelve at night.

He certainly escalated America's role in the Vietnam War. I have no doubt that the war was the determining factor in his decision not to run for reelection in 1968. When he did not run for a second full term, it surprised just about all of us in Washington. Health could have been a factor, as he had had a couple of heart attacks during his senatorial years, but I am sure the war controversy forced him to step aside.

His wife and daughters were very charming and capable. Lady Bird did a lot to bring beautification to Washington and Virginia. There is a park in Virginia near the Potomac River that bears her name. I pass it every morning on my way to work.

Lyndon Johnson was really a self-made man who had a lot of ambition. I thought he was a good president who worked hard for low-income Americans and minorities. I believe if he had run again, he would have been elected.

He could be crude when you talked to him on a personal basis, but you knew when you could say a few curse words in his presence and when not to. He was a true son of Texas and brought a lot of that with him from Texas to Washington.

I met Richard Nixon and voted for many of his programs. He was very nice to me and called me "General." He took me and other members of Congress for a cruise on his yacht, the *Sequoia* when he was battling the Watergate scandal. We cruised up and down the Potomac, and I believe we drank California red wine while he was drinking the French Red. I traveled with him on the *Sequoia* again about a month before he resigned from office. Those of us with him on that cruise advised him to fight any charges regarding his role in Watergate.

Watergate was a third-rate amateur break-in. Many of my colleagues and I thought it was some kind of dumb political operation, and we were right. But I, along with many others, never dreamed it would cause a president of the United States to resign. When the president did not destroy the tapes and the Senate was moving ahead on its hearings on Watergate, the House of Representatives started moving on impeachment in the Judiciary Committee. Peter Rodino of Rhode Island was chairman of the committee, and I believe that Trent Lott, at the time representing Mississippi's Fifth District, had just come to Congress and was on the Judiciary Committee. Since I liked President Nixon so much, I confronted Chairman Rodino in the Rayburn Gym and urged him to be fair to Nixon. He handled me well and said they were not rushing on impeachment and that President Nixon would be treated in a fair manner.

My fondness for Nixon prompted me to vote against a resolution that basically called for him to resign. I do believe if he had seen the thing through and fought the charges all the way, he might have been impeached but not proven guilty in the Senate.

The night before Nixon resigned, he had about twenty-five of his friends in Congress, Democrats and Republicans, to come to the White House. He told us he was going to resign the next day. Stunned, we asked him not to resign. We stayed with him for about an hour. He did not break down or cry. I was amazed when I left in my car from the White House grounds that there was no press or cameras confronting us about what happened in the meeting. This certainly would not be the case today.

About 2 o'clock the next morning I got a call from the White House operator saying the president wanted to speak to me. He called me General, and this time he did break down. I remember he said, "General, I let you down, I have let my friends down as President." I told him he had not let me down, and I wanted him to stay. He just said again that he had let his friends down. The next morning he announced to the nation he was resigning, and he flew off to California.

He was writing his memoirs back in California. He liked to write and did so about his own career, government in general and other subjects. I called him several times before he died and should have called him more.

I was closer to President Nixon than the other presidents I knew, with the exception of the Bushes. I did vote for most of his programs before Congress. I think he liked me personally. During his last days in the White House, we stayed in touch, and, of course, I saw him the last night he was in the White House.

I did not see Mrs. Nixon that much. As I think back on the

first ladies during my years in Congress, she was, I guess you could say, the most shy. People who knew her well, however, liked her very much.

The Nixon daughters were very charming and were an asset to their father. I would talk to Julie at various receptions before her marriage to David Eisenhower. She seemed to like Washington and living in the White House. I saw her the night before President Nixon resigned, and she was holding up well.

President Nixon was a wonderfully talented man who also had some unfortunate weaknesses. I thought he was an excellent president who got in trouble because of an amateur burglary, which I do not think he really knew about until after it happened. I never thought Watergate was worth resigning over. I believe in President Nixon's case his good qualities outweighed his bad judgment. I always thought that if President Nixon had fought to stay in office, as President Clinton did, he would have beaten the charges. If he had leveled with the American people, the whole issue would have died away.

Gerald Ford became president after President Nixon resigned. I knew President Ford fairly well because I served with him in the House when he was minority leader. Then he became vice president after Spiro Agnew resigned. I thought he did a good job as president. He had been in the Congress and knew the members and knew how to get along with the House and Senate. He was always thoughtful in his dealings with me.

When I came to Congress in January 1967, Congressman Ford

had just been elected minority leader by the Republicans in the House. He was very capable and friendly. Gerald had a good laugh, among other traits, and he would argue with you and end up his arguments with laughter. I became his friend after I had been in the Congress about a year. He knew that on some votes in the House he could get at least part of the Mississippi delegation, which consisted of Congressmen Bill Colmer of Pascagoula, John Bell Williams of Raymond, Tom Abernethy of Okalona, Jamie Whitten of Charleston, and me.

I thought Gerald was a good leader, and with his minority Republicans, he would get conservative Democrats to help on some of his programs. He had his work cut out for him, because Lyndon Johnson was president part of the time Gerald was minority leader.

My freshman class had about twelve to fourteen newly elected Democrats, and a large number of freshman Republicans were elected. The Republicans were not able to get the majority in the House, but they started gaining numbers back in the early 70s. I remember when I first got to Congress the Democrats had a majority of over a hundred, and they made it hard on Gerald Ford and his Republican leadership. It was not all smooth sailing for him with his Republican colleagues either. A few from the big cities were moderate, and he lost some of them on certain votes.

When Spiro Agnew had to resign, President Nixon looked all over the country for a replacement. After much searching, he concluded Gerald Ford was the best man to be vice president. It

took Gerald by surprise when he was offered the position. Usually a senator or cabinet member is chosen for this type of position, and we were so glad to see a House member move up to the
vice presidency.

Gerald ran a pretty sorry campaign in 1975 in an attempt to be
elected president on his own and was beaten by Jimmy Carter, a
former governor of Georgia.

President Carter was a southerner, and I tried to support his
programs whenever I could. He was not a warm man, not someone you could become buddy-buddy with; however, he was
always very nice to me. House Speaker Tip O'Neill told me that
of all the presidents he had served with, President Carter had the
quickest mind.

I thought President Carter had a capable White House staff.
Some said he brought too many Georgians to the White House,
and they knew nothing about the workings of Washington. One
of President Carter's assistants in the White House, Susan
Clough, was a good friend of mine and very nice to me whenever
she could be of help at the White House.

Jimmy Carter was a graduate of the Naval Academy and had
been a submariner. Despite his military background, President
Carter wanted to be sure that people did not think he was favor-
ing the military. I thought he should have given the military
more support. I believe that in his reelection bid in 1979, he lost
the votes of most veterans and those serving in the military.
Once in a meeting with the president and some other members of

Congress, one congressman was talking and not saying much. I remember President Carter told the congressman, "Tell me what the bottom line is in your remarks and let's move on." He did not like to waste a lot of time in meetings and speeches.

President Carter did not want the people to see him as any different from the average person. He made a practice of carrying his own luggage off of Air Force One and then into hotels. Most Americans were not impressed, and I thought that he, as president, had more important things to do than carry his own bags. I think he worried too much about what Americans thought of his image. Most of the Americans I knew wanted the president to have the special treatment that goes with the office. President Carter was a good tennis player, and he invited me to play tennis with him and two other persons, including his chief of staff, Hamilton Jordan, on the outdoor court on the White House grounds. President Carter really liked to win, and he never gave an opponent the benefit of the doubt on a close line call. I would not argue with the president of the United States, but Hamilton Jordan would on the line calls. The president always won out. After playing in the hot weather, it was nice when, between the two sets and afterwards, one of the White House stewards brought out lemonade and cookies.

Carter wanted, as all presidents do, to be reelected to a second term. I am told he thought he would be reelected, but Ronald Reagan was too good a campaigner and politician. President

Carter took his defeat very hard and could not believe that it had happened.

President Carter has been active since leaving the White House. He has a presidential office in Atlanta and works with Habitat for Humanity around the country. Like most presidents who leave office, he seemed to want to be away from Washington and went home to Georgia. Over the thirty-five years I have been in Washington, I have not seen any ex-presidents living around the city. I do believe, however, that President Carter and his family were generally well received in Washington.

President Ronald Reagan was quite a person. I did not know him as well as I knew George Bush, but President Reagan was always kind and considerate to me. Many House Democrats helped get his tax reduction bill passed. I was one of the leaders of the so-called Boll Weevils (House Democrats who supported many of Reagan's programs), and he appreciated the help we gave him.

He was always relaxed and confident in his dealings with Congress. He was very good about having members come to the White House for either breakfast or informal receptions on the White House lawn, the latter usually during the summer. Despite frequent trips to the White House, I never got to know Nancy Reagan that well. In fact, of all the first ladies in Washington during my House years, I only knew Barbara Bush well.

President Reagan enjoyed being president and did his job well, but he was not one to go out frequently to attend functions of various groups such as veterans or businesspeople. The Reagans also seemed to prefer not to get too close to the George Bushes or other prominent families of significant members of the government. He kept it pretty simple and strived to have less government and to slow government growth. He also did not interfere with the various government department heads; he let them run their departments. I thought he was an excellent president. He could make great speeches to the nation and had the ability to calm the fears of the American people.

Of the presidents I have served with, my closest relationship has been with George Bush. We came to Congress at the same time, 1967, and have been great friends ever since. On the first day of that first Congress, the Ninetieth, that we experienced, we became acquainted in the House Gymnasium in the Rayburn Building. We played paddleball, a sport new to both of us. He is a natural athlete and took up the game very quickly. We became best friends from that day forward and still are. When he was president, he told, and still tells, people that I was his best friend in the House of Representatives.

I thought he was a great president because he knew the Congress, having served two terms there himself. He had also been a World War II hero, acting ambassador to China, head of the

Republican Party, and vice president of the United States for eight years. He was the most qualified president the nation has had during my lifetime.

As president, he guided us through the Persian Gulf War and did what the United Nations Charter said we could do. He raised taxes when it had to be done, and that got him beat in his reelection bid. The outstanding economy we enjoyed in the late 90s started in the last six months of his administration. Economists will say this good time started with President Bush.

During the Persian Gulf War the Defense Department called up some of the National Guard and Reserve units but had not called up the combat arm of the Army National Guard and the combat arm of the Army Reserve. General Norman Schwartz-kopf had not requested these units, I was told. At a meeting on the Persian Gulf War with other members of Congress at the White House, I stood up and pointed out that the Pentagon had not called up these infantry brigades in the Guard and Reserve, and the president listened to me. Several weeks later the 155th Armored Infantry Brigade from Mississippi was called up to active duty. The 155th was sent to Fort Hood for some more training. Some in Mississippi got upset with me that the brigade was put on active duty to go to the Persian Gulf. Also some artillery units of the Guard were called up and ended up in combat. The 155th could have done an outstanding job if sent to the Gulf, but they never left Texas.

Since our military forces have been reduced by Congress, now when there is some small action around the world, the regulars have no choice but to use the National Guard and Reserves. I was in the actives six years and in the National Guard and Reserves for thirty years. I have always said that a man or woman is in the Reserves to help his or her country, and, given the additional money and retirement that goes with the job, no one in the Reserve should complain when his or her unit is called on to help the country.

The Persian Gulf War underscored the need for a strong Reserve program. I think it was to President Bush's credit that he listened to me, not just because of our friendship but because he knew that my background and experience qualified me to speak out on the matter.

President Bush today is one of my closest friends. He and Barbara come to Washington quite often, and we three go to St. John's Episcopal Church at Lafayette Square at 8 A.M. I see them six or seven times a year.

IV

The Montgomery GI Bill

W hen I became chairman of the Veterans' Affairs Committee, U.S. House of Representatives, in January of 1981, there were several issues I felt were critically important to those who served their country in time of need. One thing most important to me was the enactment of a GI Bill for the All-Voluntary Force. As one of the senior members of the House Armed Services Committee, I was well aware of the problems all branches of the armed forces were having in recruiting and retaining quality personnel. I intended to exert every effort in helping solve these very serious problems. We had already laid the foundation for enacting this legislation before I became chairman of the committee. Before discussing the legislative proposal, I want to comment on the background of the bill that came to bear my name.

Upon assuming the chairmanship of the committee, I asked Mack Fleming to be both the staff director and chief counsel of the committee. Mack was a great staff director and was and is a great friend. We both knew that the post-Vietnam era Veterans' Educational Assistance Program (VEAP) was not working. Few participated or used their benefits. The Montgomery GI Bill set a termination date for VEAP entitlement but not for benefits and created a new education assistance program.

Mack played a key role in getting the legislation bearing my name enacted into law. I asked him and other members of the committee staff to meet personally with all branches of the service and to develop an education plan that would 1) provide a new educational assistance program to aid in the readjustment of members of the armed forces to civilian life after their separation from military service; 2) promote and assist the All-Volunteer Force program, the Total Force Concept of the All-Volunteer Force program, and the Total Force Concept of the Armed Forces by establishing a new program of educational assistance to aid in the recruitment and retention of highly qualified personnel for both the active and reserve components of the armed forces; and 3) give special emphasis to providing educational assistance to aid in the retention of personnel in the armed forces. The plan had to include benefit incentives that would enhance the ability of all branches of service to recruit and retain quality personnel. This was critical at the time in that more than half of recruits coming into the Army were in the lowest mental category.

We spent many months in discussing these issues with the Army, Navy, Air Force, Marines, and Coast Guard. In the late 70s and early 80s the Army was having major problems in recruiting quality personnel. Disciplinary problems were mounting. The Air Force had fewer recruiting problems but were experiencing severe difficulties in retaining personnel. The Navy had similar problems.

Our plan was designed to help all of the armed forces. We held meetings in the Pentagon, on Capitol Hill, and in various other places so that each branch of service could lay out its needs. We were most fortunate to have General Max Thurmond heading the Army Recruiting Command, one of the very best leaders in the Army. Among other things he developed the slogan "Be all that you can be," which caught on like wildfire. General Thurmond also stressed the need to provide educational benefits for the All-Voluntary Force. He strongly believed that education was the best recruiting incentive the Army and all other branches of service could offer, and he worked with me in developing a GI Bill that would help solve many of the armed forces' problems.

I am very proud of the Montgomery GI Bill, which has helped more than 2.5 million young service men and women in the armed forces continue their education. It took almost five years to get the bill through the Congress. The bill provides benefits to those serving on active duty and, for the first time, provides educational benefits for the National Guard and Reserves. Under today's Total Force, it is absolutely essential that the Guard and Reserves be given similar benefits as those on active duty. While previous GI bills had my support, I believed we could do better and needed to do better for the sake of the men and women who are out front in defense of our nation.

I introduced the bill initially in 1981. The bill provided basic benefits of $300 a month for a maximum of thirty-six months based on three years active duty or two years of active duty plus four years in the Selected Reserves. These benefits would be paid by the Veterans Administration. The basic monthly benefit could be raised up to an additional $400 a month under certain conditions, the extra money to be paid by the Department of Defense. This benefit would be paid to any individual who has a skill or specialty, as designated by the Secretary of Defense, in which there is a critical shortage of personnel. As I write this, the Congress is raising monthly benefits to about $800 in January 2002, $900 in October 2002, and $985 in October 2003.

Another important part of the bill as introduced would have authorized certain members of the armed forces to transfer entitlement to dependents. This transfer provision was designed to help retain individuals designated by the Secretary of Defense as having a skill or specialty for which there is a critical shortage of personnel. There is a good chance the 107th Congress will address the transferability issue in the defense bill for 2002.

Finally, the bill would have established a Pre-service Educational Assistance Program to encourage enlistment in the active-duty components of the armed forces and in units of the Selected Reserve. Under the bill the secretary concerned could enter into pre-service educational assistance agreements with individuals who agree to perform a specified period of obligated service on active duty or in the Selected Reserve. The bill contained several other sections that established guidelines and parameters.

I first introduced the bill in the Ninety-seventh Congress, and it was jointly referred to the Veterans' Affairs and Armed Services Committees. These committees held nineteen hearings, including twelve by the Armed Services Subcommittee on Personnel and Compensation and seven by the Veterans' Affairs Subcommittee on Education, Training, and Employment. Included in the seven were two field hearings, and the two subcommittees also held one joint hearing. Witnesses from across the military complex spectrum testified. The committees also heard testimony from representatives of the armed forces, Department of Defense, Veterans Administration, national service veterans' organizations, military associations, educational associations and institutions, and the Congressional Budget Office. The House Veterans' Affairs Committee reported the bill (H.R. 1400) to the House in 1981, the year in which I introduced the bill; however, since it was jointly referred to the Armed Services Committee, it was not reported by that committee until late 1982.

Why was the bill delayed a year? It came as a shock to me that some leaders in both the House and Senate were opposed to the enactment of a GI Bill for the All-Volunteer Force. There was not the strong support I expected of the leadership in the House Armed Services Committee. The leadership wanted to know where we would find the money to fund the program. The answer was clear when the president informed everyone of his intent to increase the defense budget by several billion dollars a year. With the unanimous approval of the House Veterans' Affairs Committee in 1981 and the help of many members of the House Armed Services Committee, the latter committee reported the bill to the House in 1982. We requested a rule to bring the bill to the floor of the House of Representatives for consideration and vote. The rule was not granted before the Ninety-seventh Congress adjourned sine die.

In the Ninety-eighth Congress, which convened in 1983, I reintroduced H.R. 1400 on February 1. It contained the same language as the bill I introduced in 1981. Three other bills were also introduced that would establish educational programs for veterans and active-duty members of the military. Most of the provisions of the other bills were very similar to those contained in my original bill, H.R. 1400. Again, my bill was jointly referred to the Veterans' Affairs and Armed Services Committees. It should be noted here that although the bill originated in the Veterans' Affairs Committee, a secondary purpose of the proposed legislation was to assist the secretaries of the armed forces in recruiting and retaining the very best personnel. In addition, the secretary of defense was responsible for paying for the "kickers" for those in critical skilled positions, so the bill had to be considered by Armed Services as well as our own committee. Joint referrals make the process more complex, and the time to move the proposed legislation takes much longer. Hearings were held in Biloxi, Mississippi, in March and again in April.

On May 4, 1983, the Subcommittee on Education, Training, and Employment recommended H.R. 1400 to the full Veterans'

Affairs Committee. The full committee reported the bill to the House on May 10 as Report 98-185, entitled the "Veterans' Educational Assistance Act of 1983."

Since the Armed Services Committee was not moving H.R. 1400, during the consideration of H.R. 5167 (Department of Defense Authorization Act of 1985), I amended the proposal, adding the provisions of H.R. 1400 as reported to the House by the Veterans' Affairs Committee. On June 1, 1984, H.R. 5167 passed the House with the provisions of H.R. 1400. The measure had overwhelming bipartisan support. Unfortunately, the leadership in the Senate was not very supportive of the education provisions contained in H.R. 5167, which had passed the House. Senators William Cohen of Maine and Bill Armstrong of Colorado, along with twenty cosponsors, tried without success to pass a version similar to H.R. 5167. Given the unfavorable position of the leadership of the Senate Armed Services Committee, the bill did not pass the Senate with the GI Bill provisions contained in the House-passed Bill.

It is important to note that the Senate did pass a bill. The bill had to go to a House-Senate Conference to work out the differences in the two bills. It is also important to remember that when the conferees were named in the House, the Veterans' Affairs Committee had far fewer conferees than the Armed Services Committee. I immediately asked the speaker of the House to name additional conferees from the Veterans' Affairs Committee so that each committee would have the same number. I did not want to be outvoted by the Armed Services Committees of the House or Senate. The speaker permitted me to do this, and doing so saved the bill in conference with the other body.

The House and Senate conferees met to work out differences between the two bodies on the Authorization Bill. What a conference it was—unlike any I had ever attended during my tenure in the House. The late senator from Texas John Tower was chairman of the conference on the Defense Authorization Bill, which included the GI Bill. Since the GI Bill had cleared both the House Veterans' Committee and the Armed Services Committee, the education provisions had to be resolved in the Defense Authorization Bill. Senator Tower was opposed to the GI Bill benefit package, viewing it as unnecessary. Congressman Tom Foley of Washington was Speaker of the House during these times and supported the GI Bill.

Senator Tower scheduled the GI education provisions as the last item on the conference agenda. This meant that the conferees would have met for hours working out the many other differences between the House and Senate before getting to the education part of the bill. The hour was late, and the members were very tired. As I recall we began discussing the GI Bill provisions late in the day—so late that Senator Tower recessed the conference so that everyone could eat supper and he could try to round up some more votes that supported his position. In the meantime, I had the Army bring in some MREs (Made Ready To Eat), and we did not recess.

After supper we began negotiations again. Every time Senator Tower called for a roll call vote, I was confident and would take the proxies given to me and vote them. Each time the House would prevail. After many votes I began to get a little irritated with the other body and asked for permission to speak. I suggested to Chairman Tower that maybe I had made a mistake in the logo we designed for the GI Bill we supported. Rather than a logo consisting of a cap and gown, I should have placed the education provisions in a cylinder with a nose cone at the front and a fuse in the back so that it looked like a missile that would destroy a convoy of ammo trucks and then it would pass. I reminded everyone that education benefits for military personnel would enhance their lives upon leaving service. In addition, I reminded them that all military leaders were in agreement that GI Bill benefits would be the very best incentive for recruiting and retaining quality personnel.

Unfortunately, the Senate leadership was not willing to agree with the position of the House. Before we could get any positive move by Senator Tower, we had to accept his very strong opinion that any service member who participated in the GI Bill program could do so only by agreeing to have $100 per month for twelve months deducted from his or her pay. Such requirement was not in the legislation passed by the House.

While the conference debates continued on, I spoke in the House on July 31, 1984, regarding the need for a good bill. I said, "The Brookings Institution reports that the declining pool of eligible military recruits may force a return to the draft in the 1990s if we are to maintain projected force levels in our military. In my opinion, we can deter the need for a draft by passing the GI Education Bill now pending in the DOD [Department of Defense] Conference Committee. The GI Bill is strongly supported by the House of Representatives as you voted for it in the Military Authorization Bill. We believe it can provide the kind of incentive necessary to recruit and retain qualified young men and women for our armed forces. The GI Bill offers more than just bonus pay to new recruits. It offers an opportunity for higher education that will mean better jobs, higher incomes, and security. For the sake of America's security, it's time to pay attention to the signals. Recruitment will be tough in the new future. It makes more sense to give the all-volunteer system a real opportunity to work than to reinstate the draft. The new GI Bill is that opportunity. I would hope that Congress has the foresight to use it."

With the strong support of Senators William Cohen of Maine, Bill Armstrong of Colorado, Alan Cranston of California, and my fellow conferees from both the Armed Services and Veterans' Affairs Committees of the House, we prevailed in conference. About 2:00 A.M., Senator Tower gave up, and I thought we had reached full agreement on the new permanent GI Bill for the All-Voluntary Force.

After resolving all issues between the two bodies, the staff of both committees in the House and Senate met with the legislative counsels of the House and Senate to work out all technical aspects of the bill. To the surprise of the House staff, the Senate staff of the chairman and ranking member of the Senate Armed Services Committee insisted that their members had only agreed to accept the education amendments for a three-year test period. That was news to me when my staff director called me at home with this information. At that late hour, with the conference agreement going to the floor for a vote the next day, there was little chance, if any, of calling the members back to resolve the issue.

I asked my staff director, Mack Fleming, to meet with the House Armed Services Committee staff so that we could be assured that the position taken by the Senate Armed Services staff was totally wrong and that they would support us in making the GI Bill permanent. As I recall, Mack informed the Senate staff, "tonight you may have won the battle on this issue, but you will lose the war when Chairman Montgomery moves to correct it." So the All-Volunteer Force GI Bill became law, but, unfortunately, limited to three years. Nonetheless, I was very confident that the Bill would be made permanent within the so-called three-year test period.

Even though it was a struggle, differences between the House and Senate were worked out, and a suitable bill was passed. President Ronald Reagan signed the bill into law, and it became Public Law 98-525. The law was more commonly known as the Educational Assistance Act of 1984 until my name was attached to it. Subsequent legislation, as mentioned below, has updated the bill, and I am pleased that three Mississippians, Congressmen Chip Pickering, Ronnie Shows, and Roger Wicker are working to expand the benefits.

In 1987 I introduced a bill, H.R. 1657, to make the bill permanent. Section 1 of that bill proposed elimination of temporal restrictions on the availability of the new GI Bill. What I proposed was changing the language of the original bill to state that the provisions therein would be initiated after June 30, 1985, and remove the ending date of June 30, 1988. In other words, I intended to make the program permanent, as we thought Members had agreed to in the 1984 conference. The original bill was threatened when President Reagan sought to eliminate it in his fiscal year 1987 budget, even before the three years had expired. I felt compelled to fight for the bill because it was working. I fondly recall how the legendary Senator Strom Thurmond spoke in favor of protecting the bill. He said simply, "The program is a pilot program and should be allowed to run its course." I wanted the course to be a long one, longer than three years. It took some negotiations and maneuvering to get that done, but we did succeed in making the bill permanent.

Out of the committee work on the bill came a nice surprise and high honor for me. I was most pleased when Congressman Lane Evans of Illinois, a senior member of the committee, introduced an amendment to the bill to make the program permanent. Before reporting H.R. 1085, the Veterans' Affairs Committee accepted Congressman Evans's amendment to name the GI Bill the Montgomery GI Bill Act of 1984. It has become known as the Montgomery GI Bill. In offering his amendment, Congressman Evans commented on my role in the proposed legislation. He said, "You had the vision to conceive the New GI Bill. You had the courage to fight for it against strong and committed opposition. You had the leadership needed to succeed. It has done what you said it would and even more."

My friend Congressman Gerry Solomon of New York further commented, "Anyone who knows Sonny knows that he has put his heart and soul into this program. His enthusiasm is infectious. You would be hard pressed to find a program with a broader or more loyal base of support—in the Congress, at the Pentagon, among educators, and among the families of young recruits who welcome an opportunity to go to college." Needless to say, I was quite flattered. Such comments coming from my colleagues made the fight for the bill all the more worthwhile.

On June 30, 1988, the three-year anniversary of the bill, I spoke on the floor of the House. These were my remarks. "Mr. Speaker, tomorrow marks the third anniversary of the Montgomery GI Bill. Three years ago, new active duty recruits and members of the National Guard and selected Reserves were first offered the opportunity to participate in this new educational assistance program for the All-Volunteer Force. Since that time, over 514,000 young men and women on active duty have signed up for the GI Bill. Over 90,000 members of the selected Reserves have gone to school under the program. As originally enacted in 1984, the GI Bill was established as a three-year test. But for the support and commitment to this program on the part of my colleagues in the Congress, today would mark the ending of this program. The following participation rates for May 1988, clearly demonstrate the popularity of the GI Bill: Army—91.9%, Navy—72.1%, Air Force—75.7%, Marine Corps—74.0%, and DOD wide—80.4%. Additionally, I want to point out that the basic pay reductions, which are required under the Montgomery GI Bill–Active Duty, have returned over 462 million dollars to the Treasury. On behalf of the hundreds of thousands of young men and women who are now able to further their education under the GI Bill, I want to thank all of my colleagues for ensuring that the program is still alive and well."

I put out a press release in which I said that Congress had "taken a giant step toward strengthening the recruitment and retention of qualified men and women for the all-volunteer armed forces by approving a GI education package as part of the 1985 defense authorization bill." I went on to say that I thought "the education package is the most important part of the bill because of the benefits it will bring not only to the armed forces, but society as well." I pointed out that, looking ahead to the early 1990s, "the pool of eligible young recruits will be greatly diminished. To keep up with current personnel needs, the military will need to recruit one out of every two non-college males in order to keep up. Add to that an improving U.S. economic picture, which will make available new and better-paying jobs, and you can see that recruitment could become a big problem. The same is true for retention of these bright young men and women, who see a larger paycheck from employment in the private sector." I concluded my comments with, "I am optimistic about the possibilities created by passage of this education package. It will help ensure a strong national defense and provide educational opportunities for our young men and women at the same time." I believe time has proven my optimism to be justified.

Though the bill has had dynamic results, getting it passed proved to be more difficult than I had imagined. During all the negotiations, when some members like Senator John Tower were giving me a hard time, Congressman Ron Dellums of California, a senior member of the House Armed Services Committee, pitched in and helped me out. He did so because he knew a GI Bill for the All-Voluntary Force would be the greatest incentive for recruiting the best men and women for all branches of service. In addition, he knew the bill would greatly benefit minority members of the service. Senator Bill Cohen of Maine also came to my aid. He was one of the strongest advocates in helping move the bill forward in the Senate. The late Bill Nichols, former member of the House and a senior member of the House Armed Services Committee also stayed with me all the way in the lengthy conference we had with the Senate. We couldn't have been successful without their outstanding leadership and support. Lane Evans of Illinois and Bob Stump of Arizona, a close friend of mine for many years, were also strong supporters of the GI Bill. They have worked hard to raise the benefit levels, and they have been successful. Lane is now the ranking member of the House Veterans' Affairs Committee, and Bob is the chairman of the House Armed Services Committee.

Monetary benefits paid to service personnel using the GI Bill who served on active duty for the required length of time have totaled $6,706,638,900. For the Guard and Reserves benefits have come to $1,232,959,600, for a total of $7,939,598,500. The requirement that active duty service personnel pay $100 per month for twelve months has brought into the Treasury about $2,708,505,000.

Over the years I have received many compliments and expressions of thanks for my role in getting the GI Bill enacted into law. Admiral J. M. Boorda, U.S. Navy, wrote, "I would like to thank you as the author of our Montgomery GI Bill for your tremendous support of our people over your congressional career." Rear Admiral Bob Spiro Jr., U.S. Naval Reserve, said, "I much enjoyed working with you on modifications to the GI Bill of Rights." General C. C. Krulak, U.S. Marines, wrote me, "I can assure you that your legacy will continue to benefit our men and women in uniform through the Montgomery GI Bill." An Army veteran from Carthage, Mississippi, told me, "Your Montgomery GI Bill provided education for millions of veterans. I know that this makes you proud."

Jim Dykstra, who provided wonderful support and leadership working for Senator Cohen in the Senate on this measure, and who was later an assistant to Congressman Stephen Horn of California, made comments in later years that I really appreciated. He said, "Clearly, the most unforgettable part of my time on Capitol Hill will be the House-Senate conference of a decade ago when you and Senator Cohen faced down some of the most formidable opposition I've encountered in my years here and succeeded in including the Montgomery GI Bill as part of the Defense Authorization Bill. You can take pride in knowing that, as a direct result of your unflagging efforts, some two million young men and women have been afforded the opportunity to receive federal assistance for their higher education in return for their service to the military."

People come up to me and say, thanks, I got my bachelor's degree, master's, or Ph.D. through the Montgomery GI Bill. They write me too, with comments such as these from a servicewoman retired from the Air Force: "I want to join with the many veterans who have benefited from your presence in the Congress over the years and more specifically from the Montgomery GI Bill. Thank you for keeping faith in us." A former Marine wrote me, "You will be remembered for the Montgomery Bill which has been a tremendous boon for servicemen. Having enlisted in the Corps with only a high school diploma, I eventually acquired a B.S. and M.A. through similar GI Bills during and after WWII. All of that academic success occurred during active service, and I am extremely grateful for the opportunity." Such feedback makes my day.

The Marine's comments show how important veterans' benefits are and underscore my conviction that aid needs to be available always in order to help individuals who in turn defend their country. A friend of mine put it well when he said, "I think your work in reinstituting the GI Bill, now appropriately the Montgomery GI Bill, is the most significant in the national security arena. Because of your foresight and ability to make things happen legislatively, the U.S. military has been able to recruit the remarkably talented individuals that now make it clearly the best military force in the world. There is no way they could have achieved these kinds of results without the Montgomery GI Bill." I do not share this to pat myself on the back but to illustrate why I thought the bill was so essential.

I especially appreciate the sentiments expressed in a June 1, 1987, editorial in the *Air Force Times*. I quote the entire editorial, which I think, sums up my own views so well:

> The new GI Bill educational assistance program came into being as a three-year test, a short fuse that many expected would blow away the idea on or before the expiration date, June 30, 1988. Instead, the program weathered controversy, sprang to unanticipated heights of popularity and finally won bipartisan support for a permanent legislative lease on life. Sporadic earlier

moves to limit the aid to a three-year continuation of the test col-
lapsed before a groundswell of reports showing the success the
program was achieving. Politicians, as much as the rest of us, recognize that it pays to go with a winner. It became clear a few years
ago that the services had a loser on their hands in the Veterans'
Education Assistance Program, known as VEAP. The lawmakers
must be accorded a full measure of collective credit for leaping
from the failure of VEAP to the success of the new, completely
restructured program. This recent addition to a long line of GI Bill
school aid programs promises to be a wise investment for the
nation, paying immeasurable dividends to society, to the military
services and eventually to the federal Treasury, as well as to the
service members who enroll. The gains to society are both tangi-
ble and intangible. By making the aid available, we avert the
tragic human waste that occurs when people of high potential
lack the funds to continue their education. We produce better,
more fulfilled citizens. The aid programs help the services attract
the kind of troops they need and demand—bright people who are
easy to train, who perform well in difficult assignments and
whose behavior is generally exemplary. Finally, most recipients
of assistance greatly increase their earning power. They consequently make larger income tax payments throughout their lifetime, a "revenue enhancement" that some authorities have cal-
culated at triple the sums invested in educational aid. Most
people, no doubt, will go on calling the program the New GI Bill.
However, the permanent legislation was officially—and appropri-

ately—renamed the "Montgomery GI Bill Act" to recognize the pre-eminent role played by Rep. G. V. Montgomery, D-Miss., chairman of the House Veterans' Affairs Committee and a senior member of the House Armed Services Committee. Actually, there are now three rather different programs, one for active-duty recruits, one for the reserve components and one that will allow those eligible for Vietnam-era GI Bill benefits to combine entitlements under both programs if they are still on active duty after 1989. We say three cheers for all three.

And I say three cheers for the person or persons who composed this editorial.

We must not rest on our laurels. Congress needs to increase the benefits, and Congressman Shows of Mississippi has recently introduced legislation to upgrade benefits. Members of Congress, veterans, and military organizations met on the Capitol steps on March 1, 2000, to call for increasing the benefits in the Montgomery GI Bill. Among those speaking in favor of enhancing the benefits were Chairman Jack Quinn, Congressmen Bob Filner, Dave Bonior, Chairman Bob Stump, John Dingell, J. D. Hayworth, and Lane Evans.

There have been efforts in the 107th Congress (2001) to further enhance benefits and to restore some promised benefits to Vietnam-era veterans. Other proposed legislation would make it easier to use educational assistance as provided by the bill in areas that would lead to employment in high-technology industries. Other efforts include adjustments of the annual determination of the rate of basic benefits and permitting the transfer of entitlement to educational benefits provided by the GI Bill.

I also want to comment on the recent report of the Congressional Commission on Service Members and Veterans Transition Assistance, chaired by Anthony Principi, who is now head of the Department of Veterans Affairs. This commission was set up in 1996 to review veterans' benefits. For Montgomery GI Bill participants, the commission recommended increases in monthly payments and provisions of accelerated payments for certain types of education. The commission further recommended repealing the $100 monthly contribution by GI Bill participants to ease pressure on our service men and women. The commission made many other excellent recommendations, and I applaud these efforts, as well as those of current members of Congress, to continue enhancing benefits for those who defend our country.

With this new war on terrorism, I am more convinced than ever that we must have quality young people on the front lines and that we must reward them adequately for their efforts. With the cost of education going up in colleges about 10 percent a year, the GI Bill benefits must be increased. Friends like Bob Stump of Arizona, Lane Evans of Illinois, Cliff Steams of Florida, Bob Filner of California, and others in the House continue to work to increase these benefits. In the Senate, Minority Leader Trent Lott and his staff assistant Eric Womble have also worked to enhance the program. Senator Arlen Specter of Pennsylvania and Senator

Jay Rockefeller of West Virginia are strong supporters of the bill. Others who have stood firmly behind this issue are Senator Nighthorse Campbell of Colorado, who served in the House, Senate Majority Leader Tom Daschle, Senator Edward Kennedy, former senator and secretary of defense Bill Cohen, Senator Max Cleland, and former senators Alan Cranston and Alan Simpson. There are many others too. I record these names to give an idea of how support for our veterans spreads across a wide ideological spectrum of representatives and senators. All have contributed in so many ways to increasing benefits while at the same time reducing or eliminating any burdens on veterans who participate in the program.

About 55 percent of those eligible for the GI Bill are using the benefits. We need to raise the monthly benefit substantially so that more will take advantage of this aid. In addition, rather than the regular CPI automatic index, Congress should have an index based on increased cost of education. Finally, Congress should consider and act on the recommendations of the Congressional Transition Commission, especially the elimination of payroll deductions of our veterans who want to participate.

When the economy is good and they can get fairly good jobs, veterans tend not to use the benefits in the GI Bill. They should do both—take the job but continue the education. When the economy is not good, veterans usually enroll in an education program using the benefits. As I have said—perhaps "preached" would be a better word—we must raise the stipend so more veterans will take advantage of the program. In return, these individuals will get college degrees. They will be able to move into better jobs for themselves and for the welfare of their families.

The GI Bill after World War II transformed this country into a much better educated nation. That bill gave us industrialists, doctors, engineers, lawyers, teachers, and businesspeople. This is what the Montgomery GI Bill is doing for our young service members and veterans, but we must continue to make the program more and more attractive. We have come to expect the best from our military forces. In turn we should provide those young men and women the best in benefits.

In an evaluation summary of the Montgomery GI Bill conducted by Klemm Analysis Group of Washington, D.C., August 17, 2000, the World War II GI Bill of Rights has been deemed extremely successful and to have greatly influenced the face of American society today. Michael J. Bennett, in his book, *When Dreams Came True*, and Peter Drucker, author of *Post-Capitalist Society*, both identify the GI Bill as a milestone of the twentieth century. Some historians have said that the World War II GI Bill was one of the best legislative programs ever to have become law. We must strive to do as much for veterans of the All-Voluntary Force and for those who served in other conflicts since. In many ways, the future of our country is as solid as the status of our military. To keep that status solid, we must draw the best and brightest into military service, and I do believe the GI Bill is a key element, perhaps the key element, in our efforts to do so.

V

The Department of Veterans Affairs

Back in the early 1980s, Congressman Gerald Solomon from upstate New York and I started working to make the Veterans Administration a cabinet department. The Veterans Administration had been created as an independent agency in 1930. As a department, it would have more prestige and clout as a voice for American veterans. Congressman Solomon and I worked on this project for many years before we were finally successful. What seemed to us to be a logical step for the Veterans Administration appealed to many but not to all.

I recall that the major paper in my home state of Mississippi, the *Jackson Clarion-Ledger*, editorialized in 1987 against a cabinet-level department for veterans. The editorial caught me by surprise, and I felt a need to respond point by point. The paper claimed that such a cabinet post would not guarantee veterans any more recognition than they already had. I said that was wrong and pointed out that currently the Veterans Administration was run by bureaucrats in the Office of Management and Budget who cared little about the history and purpose of veterans' benefits. Direct VA input into OMB decisions, I argued, was either limited or disregarded entirely. I said that within the executive branch, the VA and its employees knew best how to administer resources, and, that being the case, should not the agency be a major contributor to the decisions that would affect those same resources? Should not the VA be allowed to participate in the discussion that shaped its future? Was it not time that the veterans of this country had access to their government at its highest levels, access commensurate with the immeasurable contributions and sacrifices they have made to establish and safeguard that government? Should not their representative be allowed to speak face-to-face with the president? After all, policy decisions affecting veterans should be made at the highest level of government, and granting cabinet status to the VA would guarantee that.

The paper's editor also said that the best way to keep veterans' issues before the public was to work hard through the legislative process, where adequate benefits and good programs could be implemented. My response was that making the VA a cabinet-level department did exactly what the editor recommended. With our legislation, we wanted to upgrade the VA, allowing it to participate in the legislative process by restoring its power to speak over OMB objection. I noted that the VA mission involved a broad cross section of Americans, greatly affecting the economy and representing a wide variety of domestic programs. Considering the size of the agency, its constituency and responsibilities, its long history of invaluable service to the nation, and, most important, the deference due our veterans for their service and sacrifices, upgrading the VA to cabinet level was completely war-ranted. The editor said such a move was not good policy, but I countered that it was exactly the type of policy this nation would do well to adhere to in all matters.

I was chairman of the Veterans' Committee in the House, and Gerry Solomon was the ranking Republican of that committee. In those positions, we had some influence in moving this bill for-ward. It took several years of trying before we got the legislation out of the House Administration Committee because of the opposition of Jack Brooks of Texas, who chaired that committee. Chairman Brooks liked me personally, but he was very party-ori-ented, and, though I was a fellow Democrat, he did not particu-larly want to support anything that Solomon, a Republican, was sponsoring. I worked on Brooks for a couple of years. He had been a Marine in World War II and was a full colonel in the Marine Reserve, and that gave leverage. Finally he relented and moved the bill out of his committee for the full House to vote on.

All the great veterans' organizations got on board and lobbied members of the House to support the bill. One of the arguments I used in speaking for the bill was that for years the veterans had to go to the back door of the White House because the VA was an agency; by becoming a Veterans Department, they could now go in the front door of the White House. This was literally true in the sense that when an agency becomes a department, the head of that department becomes a secretary and attends cabinet meet-ings at the president's table in the White House.

When we got going on the bill, we had two versions, H.R. 3471 in the House and S. 533 in the Senate. Ultimately the Senate accepted the House version. On November 17, 1987, the House approved the bill by a lopsided vote of 399-17. I talked about the results of that vote in my December 1987 report to my Third District constituents in Mississippi. I assured them that President Ronald Reagan strongly supported the bill and that we expected the Senate to pass the bill in the near future. I remarked that the bill's supporters thought this a step long overdue. Veterans' programs were too important to be left to midlevel bureaucrats in the OMB. After all, veterans and their families at that time constituted one-third of the population of the United States. That meant a significant number of people in our country relied on hospitals, pensions, and insurance programs run by the VA. In light of that, it seemed reasonable that the VA ought to have access directly to the president and other members of his cabinet.

I further added, in answer to some critics, that making the VA a cabinet-level operation would not mean the formation of yet another huge bureaucracy in Washington. The cost would be minimal, since the VA already was the federal government's second largest agency and employed more people than all other agencies with the exception of the Department of Defense. At the time, it had the fifth largest budget of all agencies, some $28 billion. The VA ran the largest hospital system in the free world, with, at the time, some 172 hospitals, 229 out-patient clinics, 117 nursing homes, and 189 veterans' counseling centers. It also operated, and still does, one of the largest life insurance programs in the world and directs one of the government's largest home loan guaranty programs.

The point was that this issue was not about adding to what the VA already had in place; it was about providing veterans, through the VA, with a place on the first team of government— the president and his cabinet. The only cost involved would be making new signs to read "Department of Veterans Affairs."

Many military and veterans groups vocally supported us, including the Veterans of Foreign Wars, the Disabled American Veterans, the Paralyzed Veterans of America, Blinded Veterans Association, Jewish War Veterans, Catholic War Veterans, the Association of the U.S. Army, the Military Order of Purple Hearts, Vietnam Veterans of America, and the American Ex-Prisoners of War.

On July 12, 1988, the Senate Committee on Governmental Affairs sent H.R. 3471 to the full Senate by unanimous consent. The Senate, after minor modifications, passed the bill in lieu of its own bill by a yea-nay vote of 84-11. In August of that year, the House disagreed with Senate amendments and requested a conference, and I was appointed one of the conferees. We hammered out the differences, and on October 6 the House agreed to the conference report by voice vote; on October 18, the Senate followed suit.

During the House debate on the conference report, I reiterated some of my previous arguments to counter continuing concerns of a few about the cost of this bill. I pointed out that the VA already had its 240,000 employees in place. Yes, we would have to change some signs, and some letterheads would have to be revised, and a few additional secretaries would be added, but other than these relatively minor costs, this law would not have any kind of major impact on the government's budget. I could not resist pointing out also that we were only doing something that should have been done years ago, and certainly we should have done it before we created four other cabinet-level departments.

I said, too, that if we passed the bill, the news would produce much cheering; old veterans would be mighty proud. I said, "Veterans have served their country well throughout our Nation's history and we owe them a debt of gratitude for their service. They have earned the right to be represented in the highest councils of the land." I thanked several people who had stuck by this idea, and I especially mentioned Gerry Solomon, pointing out that he had probably worked more and harder for this bill than anyone. I also mentioned a longtime Senate supporter of such a bill as this—Strom Thurmond of South Carolina.

I acknowledged to my House colleagues that we did not get everything we wanted during the conference with representatives of the Senate. But, I said, "In the spirit of compromise, we are in agreement with the bill. In due time we will examine the effect of some of the changes to see whether they have adversely affected the provision of services and benefits to veterans, and will propose modification or elimination of those that interfere with the accomplishment of the new department's most vital function." By "vital function" I meant, of course, service to veterans.

On October 25, President Reagan signed the bill into law, and it became Public Law Number 100-527. The president, a veteran himself, enjoyed this victory as much as supporters of the bill in Congress. We had a big celebration at Fort McNair in Washington, where the president did the actual signing, and Congressman Solomon and I each got signature pens, as the president followed a presidential tradition of using several pens to sign a bill.

The official title of the bill was the "Department of Veterans Affairs Act." The bill redesignated the Veterans Administration under that title and said that the head of the department would be the secretary of veterans affairs, to be appointed by the president with the advice and consent of the Senate. The principal officers of the department, in addition to the secretary, were to be the deputy secretary, the chief medical director, chief benefits director, and director of National Cemetery System. The bill also provided other secretarial positions at lower levels.

We redesignated the Department of Medicine and Surgery as the Veterans Health Services and Research Administration; the Department of Veterans Benefits became known as the Veterans Benefits Administration. The bill further created an Office of the General Council and the Office of the Inspector General. From these examples, you can see that we did not attempt to overhaul the VA but merely tried to adjust it to a new title and do some slight restructuring. The bill went into effect on March 15, 1989.

Gerry Solomon and I had at last realized our goal of a Department of Veterans Affairs, and now our veterans, symbolically and also in a real sense, had access to the front door of the White House. In my view the department has been a total success, and when George Bush was elected president, he offered me the position of secretary of the department. I thought about it for several days, and then I turned it down. I liked being a member of Congress, and, if confirmed, I would, of course, have had to resign from the body I had had the honor of serving in since being elected in 1967. The secretary job was a guarantee for only four years, and I wanted to be actively involved in public service for longer than that.

VI

Americans Missing in Action in Southeast Asia

The Vietnam War left a tragic legacy for our country, and no one aspect of that war has been more controversial and emotional than the fate of American soldiers missing in action. I went to South Vietnam twelve times during the war years, and after the war ended, I visited North Vietnam four times. During those visits, I came to the conclusion that the Congress needed to investigate and report on our missing men.

In 1975, I convinced my colleagues in the House of Representatives to set up a Select Committee on Americans Missing in Action in Southeast Asia. To establish such a committee required a vote of the entire House, and when the vote came, a large majority supported the measure. We were given some $350,000 to run the committee and hire staff.

We had only nine people on the committee, which I chaired, but I believe we all did a good, thorough job and came up with a factual report. Other members of the committee included Henry Gonzalez of Texas, John Joseph Moakley of Massachusetts, Patricia Schroeder of Colorado, Tom Harkin of Iowa, Jim Lloyd of California, Paul N. McCloskey Jr. of California, Benjamin A. Gilman of New York, and Tennyson Guyer of Ohio. I feel obliged to mention our capable staff too. J. Angus MacDonald served as staff director and his assistants included Henry Kenny, Job Dittberner, Shirley Ann Fulp, John Burke, and Kathleen Ann Kane.

Before going on to a review of the committee's work, I need to state up front that a majority of the committee believed that no Americans were still being held captive in Southeast Asia. There were, however, several who voted not to close the investigations and who wrote minority reports in the final report to the House Veterans' Committee. After a fifteen-month study, the committee was convinced that no Americans were still being held alive as prisoners in Indochina or elsewhere, as a result of the war in Indochina. The work we did, and the follow-up action since, has led us to a point where I believe fewer than five Americans are still being classified by our government as missing. I know also that since we wrote our report, no Americans have walked out of Southeast Asia and said they had been held captive.

We knew about a deserter named Garwood who left our American forces during the war and joined the North Vietnamese or the Viet Cong. He just left the American lines during the war and walked over to the North Vietnamese. Later he used loud speakers in an attempt to get other Americans to come over and join him. But no one ever did, and at the end of the war, he stumbled back into the American forces several months after peace had been struck. Our country did try him, but nothing came of it, and he was not put in jail. He should have been locked up for deser-

Sonny's senior portrait (Mississippi State University), 1943

George H. W. Bush and Sonny,
circa 1980s

Sonny with John C. Stennis

Sonny, 20 September 1974

Sonny at Camp Shelby, circa 1970s

George H. W. Bush and Sonny, 20 December 1987

Sonny at six months old, 1921

Sonny with Barbara and George H. W. Bush, 2 February 1989

Sonny with the Bulldog Battalion at Homecoming, 1998

Dr. Judy Crowson, George H. W. and Barbara Bush, and Sonny,
10 December 1990

Mrs. Emily Montgomery (Sonny's mother), Sonny, and
George H. W. Bush, 10 August 1981

George H. W. Bush, Sonny, and Senator Thad Cochran of
Mississippi at Mississippi State University commencement, 1989

Dear Sonny – Memories of a great day,
but can't you get some bigger letters?

Geo Bush

George H. W. and Barbara Bush with Sonny at the Armory dedication, 10 August 1981

Sonny with soldiers at Fire Support Base Thunder III in Vietnam, 1968

Second Lieutenant Aussie S. Hearron, Specialist John Weeks, Sonny, and Specialist Michael Nowak at an artillery support base in Vietnam; 26 December 1968

Second Lieutenant Aussie S. Hearron and Sonny at Fire Support Base
Thunder III in Vietnam, 1968

General H. Norman Schwarzkopf and Sonny, circa 1990

Sonny with troops from the 199th Light Infantry Brigade's 3rd Battalion in Vietnam, 22 December 1968

Sonny with troops from the 199th Light Infantry Brigade's 2nd Battalion in Vietnam, 22 December 1968

Mrs. Emily Montgomery (Sonny's mother), Sonny, and
Ms. Mildred Terrell, 1973

Sonny and John C. Stennis at John C.
Stennis Day in Meridian, MS,
9 November 1974

Sonny on a bike at the U.S.
Capitol, 1973

Sonny in Washington, 1979

Gerald Ford and Sonny, 10 October 1974

Richard Nixon and Sonny with unidentified man

Gerald Ford and Sonny

Bill Archer, Congressman from Texas; Robin Beard,
Congressman from Tennessee; Sonny; and George H. W. Bush

Sonny and Jimmy Carter

tion. He is still living in the United States, somewhere in the Midwest, I believe.

I also must mention the cooperation our committee received from the Department of Defense, the National League of Families, the United Nations High Commissioner for Refugees, the International Red Cross and their staffs, and many family members of POWs and MIAs. Many ex-POWs talked with us, and they could not give us any names of servicemen they saw at prisons who did not come out with them.

The committee saw the following as our duties: 1) to identify and explain the crucial problems associated with the issue of missing Americans, especially addressing the possibility that some might still be alive; 2) to assure that the constitutional rights of the missing were protected; 3) to create an international and domestic atmosphere where meaningful talks could be held with those who might have important information; 4) to assess how well our government agencies had addressed the prisoner of war/missing in action issue during and after the war; and 5) to provide to Congress guidelines that might help with similar situations in the future.

Our investigation moved on three fronts. Obviously, we wanted to hold hearings that would provide an informational base on which to build. We heard from about fifty witnesses who held positions that gave them access to key details. Using this data, we held some twenty executive sessions just to evaluate what we had heard and how to use it and to hear testimony on issues too sensitive to be discussed in a public forum. Next we contacted appropriate officials of the Democratic Republic of Vietnam, the Provisional Revolutionary Government of the then two Vietnams, and the Lao Peoples' Democratic Republic. We failed to make any headway in dealing with the Cambodian government. These contacts produced many meetings both at home and in Indochina and elsewhere. Finally, we sought to track leads about the status of the missing. Most information in this area came from the National League of Families of American Prisoners and Missing in Southeast Asia. While we had no legal position to look into specific cases, we did attempt to appraise the overall aspects of possibilities of Americans still being held in captivity.

While I cannot summarize here the entire results of the committee's work, I can say that in our investigations of rumors and stories of every sort, we never found credible evidence of any Americans still living in, or being held against their will in, Laos, the two Vietnams, or Cambodia. This was not, of course, what many American families and Americans in general wanted to hear. Movies and other tales about MIAs were plentiful, and so many had romantic ideas of long-lost American soldiers suddenly being found and brought home. As I said, we found no evidence to support any such thing, and since our report was written and released, no Americans have appeared out of Southeast Asia and said that they had been held captive.

I would like to offer here some information taken from that

section of our report in which I summarized what we did and offered conclusions and recommendations. I reviewed our three-pronged approach and then went on to point out that more than seventy American citizens and dependents who had been trapped by the fall of South Vietnam were allowed to return home in 1975 and 1976, in part, I believe, because of the pressure of our investigation. I believe our work produced a meeting between Secretary of State Henry Kissinger and North Vietnamese officials to discuss the whole issue. Our committee's visit to Hanoi resulted in the remains of several American soldiers being turned over for transfer to and burial in the United States. And our investigation certainly resulted in renewed focus on and interest in the MIA issue.

Our investigation showed that 2,546 Americans never returned home from the war. This figure broke down as follows: 41 civilians (25 missing or unaccounted for and 16 presumed dead); 2,505 service people, of which 1,113 had been killed and their bodies not recovered, 631 presumed dead, 728 still officially missing, and 33 listed as POWs. Of that 33, we found that 11 had been POWs not accounted for by the enemy and 6 had been improperly classified as POWs, and that there was no evidence that the remaining 16 had been taken prisoner. We also found disparities in the record-keeping practices regarding the status of missing servicemen and women.

In other areas of the investigation, we concluded that it was possible that a very small number of deserters might have still been alive in Indochina at that time. Given that possibility, we still had to say that we had no evidence of unaccounted for MIAs/POWs that were alive. We also said, without reservation, that reports of sightings and rumors of captives originated with unreliable sources in the Southeast Asia area who largely were profiteers and opportunists taking advantage of still hopeful families.

Regarding other political and diplomatic issues intertwined with this whole controversy, we also stated some of our findings. We believed that the Paris Peace Agreement that ended the war had good provisions that addressed the POW/MIA issue. We argued, however, that the so-called quiet diplomacy practiced by the State Department before 1969 had not worked but that the "go public" campaign after that year had produced results. We especially praised the State Department for its efforts from 1973 to 1975. We further concluded that cease-fire violations had canceled out the Paris Peace Agreement as an effective tool for addressing the MIA issue. We noted that our State Department had been reluctant to make significant gestures toward the Vietnamese, but we thought that such negotiations offered the only hope for any kind of accurate accounting regarding the POW/MIA issue. We also criticized the State Department for not sharing important information with us regarding contact between our government and that of Vietnam prior to our trip to Hanoi.

We also examined the role of the Department of Defense. We noted that compared to other wars in our history, the number of

MIAs resulting from the Vietnam War was small, totaling only 4 percent of those killed in action, as opposed to 22 percent in World War II and Korea. We applauded recovery efforts by our armed forces during the war and paid tribute to the Department of Defense for its attentions to the needs of families of POWs/MIAs. On the other hand, we did criticize the DOD for mistrust it created by concealing losses resulting from action in Laos. This all produced much confusion and anger, as did variations in record keeping as reflected in DOD/MIA files and files on the same individuals kept by the Joint Casualty Resolution Center.

We then looked at how legislation had impacted governmental efforts in this area. We found that Title 37 of the United States Code, along with procedural decrees by federal courts, did an adequate job in protecting the rights of the missing and their families. All the specific situations we analyzed convinced us that constitutional and estate rights of the missing had been preserved, and we endorsed adjudication rights held by the various military departments. We criticized situations where the status of missing service people had been left in the hands of the next of kin; we thought this produced an unrealistic and unnecessary burden on next of kin. In fact we came to the conclusion that most next of kin, especially wives, wanted military authorities to do their statutory duties in dealing with these cases.

Perhaps the toughest part of our investigation was accounting for the 2,546 Americans who never came home. We came away from our work convinced that all could not be, then, or ever, accounted for. We knew that 64 cases of missing and 345 cases of those listed as killed in action had happened outside zones where enemy forces were known to be operating; therefore we could not count on the military of our former enemy to help in those cases. We also concluded that deaths at sea or in crashed airplanes or other circumstances where bodies were irrecoverable amounted to more than 400. We understood, too, the political reality that Southeast Asian governments cared little about our own lists, which classified Americans as missing. They might or might not give an accounting, but we could not force them to cooperate.

We found that the Vietnamese government undoubtedly had some information on American pilots who had been shot down over what was formerly North Vietnam, as well as other documentation regarding remains of combat victims and those who died in prisoner-of-war camps. We believed that the Laotian and Cambodian governments had information on a few Americans. The factors of time, climate, and uncertainty about sites made the finding of most remains unlikely and certainly beyond the capabilities of these governments. We figured that all these Southeast Asia governments might be able to return the remains of 150 service people. While they might have information on more, it was apparent to us that outside investigative teams would never be allowed to roam the countryside in search of evidence of the missing. The Vietnamese government in any event wanted to be paid for giving an accounting. As I recall, we did not think that the amount of money they wanted, over $3 billion, would produce the data we wanted. Furthermore, they had already taken possession of billions of dollars in American supplies when South Vietnam fell after our withdrawal. We wanted to be sure too that our government did everything possible to prevent foreign governments from extorting money from POW/MIA next of kin in exchange for information.

In our recommendations to the Department of Defense, we covered several areas. We had asked DOD to place a moratorium on case reviews during the course of our investigation, so we asked that the moratorium be lifted once we finished. We urged DOD to request pertinent files from other agencies, specifically the Joint Casualty Resolution Center and Defense Intelligence Agency, to make sure that they had all available information on cases under consideration. We also recommended that DOD review the casualty classification system and set up specific guidelines for how each case should be classified. We added that future declassifications of documents should be done with much more speed, in order to expedite the overall caseload. Beyond that, we wanted DOD to be sure that all future data regarding Vietnam is retained and that communications with Indochina governments is maintained.

We asked that the DOD centralize MIA/POW policy at the outbreak of future hostilities so that Vietnam-related problems could be avoided. In that area, we wanted DOD to improve its intelligence-gathering capabilities. We recommended that a well-trained rescue force be ready in future conflicts to help extradite prisoners. The committee felt that we had been caught unprepared in many ways for dealing with the POW/MIA issue, especially in a guerrilla war like Vietnam, and we therefore wanted solid, well-planned procedures in place when needed.

Our final DOD recommendation was that a suitable memorial with the names of all Americans unaccounted for, be placed in Arlington National Cemetery.

We sent recommendations to the State Department that included reopening cases under authority of Title 5, U.S. Code. We asked that our embassy in Vietnam continue pressure on the Laos government and the Cambodians as well. The committee felt strongly that the United States should not normalize relations with any former enemy government until all had done as much as possible to help us with additional accountings of the missing. We stated several principles that we felt must be followed: 1) the Vietnamese had a humanitarian obligation to act regardless of controversy over the Paris Peace Agreement; 2) some sort of a joint commission or liaison office should be set up in Vietnam that would facilitate the flow of information; 3) future negotiations should seek a comprehensive solution rather than piecemeal strategy; 4) negotiations should focus on future relations rather than dwelling on the past; and 5) our Department of State might consider humanitarian aid to the area but should say a definite "no!" to war reparations. We asked that the State Department confer with DOD and suggested that if our efforts failed, these agencies should bring the problem to the attention of the international community. We hoped that such institutions as the Red Cross and the United Nations might provide some leverage in our quest for more information.

To our colleagues in the House of Representatives, the committee urged immediate action to assure that what we had accomplished and the information we had gathered should not be wasted. To help in oversight of future negotiations by our government with Indochina, we urged that the International Relations Committee of the House take our report as a basis for making sure the accounting process went forward in a proper manner. We asked that records and, if needed, staff of the Select Committee be transferred to the International Relations Committee. Finally, we said to the Congress that any future concessions to these former enemy governments in return for information should certainly include safeguards assuring full compliance on this issue of accounting for our missing countrymen.

While our investigation produced no startling results such as the location of missing still alive in Indochina, we did, I hope, discredit the sensationalists who kept suggesting that some of our men were still being held in prisons. There were several American prisoner camps in North Vietnam besides the Hanoi Hilton, and our cross-checking with former prisoners, who saw Americans in different camps, indicated that every American who had been seen and had not died from disease and/or cruel treatment came out when the prisoners were released. This helped us in our efforts to get an accurate accounting. And while we did not get good cooperation from Laos, we concluded that the reason was that most Americans shot down over that country who survived were sent to North Vietnam as captives. The same situation existed in Cambodia. Vietnam was, in effect, controlling those countries that were small and bordered their country.

In September 1976, Ambassador (later vice president and president) George Bush, then chief of the United States Liaison Office in China, discussed with the committee MIA information emanating from China. Bush indicated strong doubts that China held any live Americans, and he believed that the Chinese would not condone movement by the Vietnamese of POWs into China. The ambassador was of the opinion that such movement of prisoners could not occur without the Chinese knowing, and they would certainly not approve of it. Congressman Joe Moakley of the committee helped us very much in China; he had connections with the Chinese leaders. They told us of six incidents involving U.S. aircraft lost in or near the People's Republic of China between 1952 and 1968. They offered to return the remains of two Americans, and they said they had no more information on eight other Americans lost in the Vietnam War era.

We called it as we saw it in our report, and when it was released to the Congress and the general public, the *Washington Post* editorialized that the report pulled no punches and was one of the better reports written by the Congress in several years. With a few exceptions, our fellow House members accepted our findings. Since our report was released, Congress has not set up another Select Committee, and I believe most members of Congress and most Americans have accepted that no Americans are being held captive in Indochina. Now American diplomats and regular citizens are going all over North and South Vietnam. I believe our report helped ease many minds and pushed along normalization between the United States and Vietnam.

VII

Boll Weevils

D uring President Ronald Reagan's two terms as president, we had Democrats in the House who were very conservative. Some of us felt the Democratic Leadership of the House was too liberal; most who felt that way were from the South, except for Bob Stump of Arizona (who later became a Republican). We worked with, and voted with, like-minded conservative Republicans on several issues, mostly of an economic nature. Because our group was largely southern, and because Bob Stump purchased some ties with pictures of boll weevils on them, we came to be known as "Boll Weevils." We supported many of President Reagan's proposals during both his terms.

Representative Marvin Leath of Texas has been given credit for starting the group; he, like the rest of us, was a conservative on budget and spending issues. Though I was not the leader of the Boll Weevils, I did suggest that we meet periodically in my office in the Rayburn Building, and the others agreed to do so. I had to bring in extra chairs and supplied doughnuts and coffee. We decided to meet about twice a week and focus mainly on budget issues. Phil Gramm of Texas, then a Democrat and now a Republican, said we needed to put together a budget proposal that would slow down government spending, mainly in domestic areas. We did come up with a budget and tried to submit it when the Democratic leadership presented their version, but the leadership blocked us on a rule that only let their budget be submitted.

The Democratic leadership in the House was naturally not happy about the Boll Weevils, but there was not much they could do about it. House Speaker Thomas P. "Tip" O'Neill endured us because he understood the realities of politics. I think it was a tribute to him that he did not hold a grudge against us. Most of us in the group were only voting like the large majority of our constituents wanted us to, since most of them supported President Reagan. The leadership dropped not-so-subtle hints that the Boll Weevils might lose chairmanships and rankings in committees. I did get some challenges for my chairmanship of the House Veterans' Affairs Committee, but I won in the Democratic Caucus each time. Once in the caucus I escaped losing my chairmanship by only four votes; I am sure some of my moderate and liberal colleagues were trying to send me a message.

I do not think any of us suffered any severe consequences from our party. Others in the group, in addition to myself, Stump, Leath, and Gramm, were my Mississippi colleagues David Bowen and Jamie Whitten; Joe Waggoner, Billy Tauzin, Jimmy Hayes, and Jerry Huckaby of Louisiana; Charlie Stenholm, Sam Hall,

Ralph Hall, and Kent Hance of Texas; L. F. Fountain and Charlie Whitley of North Carolina; Dan Daniel of Virginia; Ron Flippo, Tom Bevill, and Bill Nichols of Alabama; Earl Hutto of Florida; and Dawson Mathis of Georgia.

Billy Tauzin, Jimmy Hayes, and Bob Stump eventually joined the Republican Party. I think Jimmy Hayes ran for governor at one point, lost, and could not run again for the House since he had run for governor the same year of the House election. Billy Tauzin has done well as a Republican and is now chairman of the Commerce Committee, where he handles major legislation.

An area of significant support that we provided President Reagan was in reduction of the federal income tax. The president had run on a program to cut taxes, and Vice President Bush, who had served with us in the House, acted as a liaison between us and the president as we worked on this issue. The president also sent some of his aides to the Boll Weevils during the early months of his first term. They made clear that he wanted our help to pass his income tax reduction bill. He had figured out that he could not pass such a bill without some Democratic votes. As I remember, the bill cut 30 percent of income taxes over a six-year period, or a 5 percent per year cut. The economy was not very good then, and there was no surplus. We wanted the White House not to make cuts too deep, or else the government would not be able to pay its bills. At the time we were running a deficit. We agreed to a 25 percent cut over five years. This compromise passed, and I believe the Boll Weevils made passage possible.

After the passage, President Reagan invited us to the White House for a reception. He appreciated the role we played in passing a major part of his program. He continued to count on our support and had us to the White House for breakfast several times. Unlike the Democratic leadership, President Reagan understood that we could not turn our back on our constituents and our own political philosophies. He certainly considered us valuable allies, and I recall some Republicans complained, with partial humor, that they would get better treatment from the White House if they turned Democrat and became members of the Boll Weevils.

Speaker O'Neill and, after him, Speaker Tom Foley of Washington, put up with us, as I said earlier, because they needed our votes and our influence. I was the Democratic whip for Mississippi and Louisiana when O'Neill was speaker. The speaker had a whip meeting, as I recall, every Tuesday morning. I was the only Boll Weevil in the whip organization, and I felt pretty uncomfortable at times in those meetings. I can remember occasions when Democrats at the whip meeting would look at me when they talked about not getting all members of the party to vote with the speaker. The speaker knew, however, that if he pushed too hard on members like Ralph Hall and Peter Geren of Texas, Gary Condit of California, and other conservatives in the party, there could well be a massive shift to the Republicans. Those in the Republican Party, like Tauzin and Bob Stump, often tried to tease me into switching.

My chief of staff on the Veterans' Affairs Committee, Mack Fleming, and I worked hard in lining up votes in the Boll Weevil coalition, and we succeeded in strengthening the position of the group. I lost leverage, however, when the Democrats lost control of the House, and my friend Bob Stump became chairman of the committee. He had been the ranking minority member during the twelve years I chaired the committee, and we had always gotten along well, so there were no problems when he took over. Still, I missed being chairman, a position I enjoyed very much.

When George Bush became president, the Boll Weevils were not as active or as strong as when Reagan occupied the White House. The reasons for this were that some of our group, like Stump, Tauzin, and Hayes, switched to the Republicans, and also President Bush's staff simply did not apply strategies, as had Reagan, that required our cooperation as a group. That did not impact me of course. Since President Bush and I have a friendship that goes back many years, I could go to the White House or call him on the phone pretty much whenever I wanted, and he would always try to help me with whatever legislation or project I was dealing with.

The Boll Weevils faded out, and our successor group has been dubbed the Blue Dogs, a name derived from a Louisiana Cajun painter named George Rodrigue, whose artwork features blue dogs. The Blue Dogs are more liberal, in my opinion, than the Boll Weevils were. When it comes to a strong defense, however, the Blue Dogs support a strong military and will vote to fund it properly. I am pleased about that. Billy Tauzin and—before he left the Congress—Jimmy Hayes hosted early meetings of this group. Like the Boll Weevils, the Blue Dogs are not totally partisan Democrats, and they try to work with Republicans on issues of common concern. I believe that they represent more parts of the country than our group. There are other Democratic groups or caucuses in the House, but I think at the height of our power, the Boll Weevils were the most influential group of all and got more things done for the betterment of our country.

My whole time as a member of the Boll Weevils was an interesting period and in so many ways a lot of fun. Most of us who participated in the group had only been in Congress ten or perhaps fifteen years. At one time we had thirty to thirty-five representatives in the organization, enough swing votes to effect many issues. So I am proud of my time as a Boll Weevil in the Congress. For any congressman, the ideal is to do what you believe is best for your state and country. That was my reason for participating in the Boll Weevils.

VIII

Campaign Financing

Although I am still involved with politics, I no longer serve Mississippi as its congressman, and there are days that I really miss working on Capitol Hill. But there are some things I do not miss, especially running for office every two years. The problem is not the campaigning, the dinners, or the people involved in running a campaign. Rather, it is the cost of running a campaign that I do not miss—in particular, campaign financing. The money involved with campaign finance has escalated to such a level that something must be done before the political process is seriously damaged.

In my first campaign for the state senate in Mississippi in 1956, I think I spent $500–$1,000. People like Lix Fruge, a Shell Oil dealer; Dr. Bill Ray, a dentist; Champ Gibson, an attorney; Tommy Minniece, an attorney; and a few others helped me financially and in other ways during the campaign. It was a job done by and with my family and friends.

When I ran for Congress for the first time in 1966, Bob Montgomery of Canton and Al Rosenbaum of Meridian ran my campaign. Bob was my campaign manager and Al was financial chairman. We agreed that if we could raise $50,000 for the whole campaign we would have enough money, and we did raise that amount.

After our victory in the first Democratic primary we spent $35,000 of the $50,000 we had. Sadly, my opponent, Joe Bullock, was killed during the Democratic primary by a tornado that struck his car. The tornado lifted the car into the air and dropped it into a lake, killing Joe. He was a tough opponent, and I would have had a difficult time beating him; his untimely death is but one example of how unpredictable politics can be. As it turned out, I faced Mac McAllister, also from Meridian and a good friend. Even though I won the race, we remain good friends today. Mac eventually moved to Alabama and ran for governor but did not win.

As I just mentioned, when we got to the general election for Congress, we still had $15,000 remaining in our coffers. We did some television, radio, and newspaper ads, and we were still in the black, or so I thought. The week following our victory, Al and Bob added up the receipts only to discover that we owed an additional $10,000. That was big money back then, and I thought it was the end of the world. I truly believed that I would not be allowed to enter Congress owing that much money. How would we ever raise an additional $10,000? Fortunately, because I had won the seat, fund raising was easier, so we were able to eventually raise the $10,000 and honor our obligations.

My memories of spending $50,000 to run a top-flight campaign are just that, memories. Now, I observe some thirty-four years later that candidates, both incumbents and challengers, can and need to raise as much as $500,000 to $800,000 to run for the House of Representatives. Senatorial candidates must raise between two and five million dollars to vie for their state's two prestigious congressional seats. While the economy remains strong, I believe, this high-priced campaigning will continue, but when the economy slows down it will become very difficult to raise that type of money.

I can also remember when I used to solicit funds through the mail and dinners. I do not believe that I ever received more that ten or fifteen $1,000 contributions any of the times I ran for office. Instead, most donations were between $25 and $100. These days I get invitations in the mail to attend fund-raising receptions for either an incumbent or a challenger, and there is always a request for $5,000 to $10,000, whether I attend or mail the funds. And candidates, I am told, can demand big money. Maybe I made a mistake not asking for big money. I was happy with the way we handled financing my campaigns. But I should add that during my thirty years in Congress I was fortunate enough that no one ever really challenged me for my seat, so I never had any elaborate or expensive campaigns.

The campaign finance situation is not hopeless, however. As early as 1907, President Theodore Roosevelt pushed for legislation that supported public financing of federal elections. That same year Congress passed the Tillman Act that prohibited business groups from contributing to a federal candidate's campaign fund. In 1947, the Taft-Hartley Act was passed and permanently banned the contributions by unions and corporations in general elections. These restrictions were later expanded to primaries and conventions.

More legislation regarding campaign financing was passed throughout the twentieth century. But in 1972, the 1971 Federal Election Campaign Act (FECA) was made law and has stood as the cornerstone for campaign financing legislation. I can recall when the issue was being debated on the House floor. Fellow congressmen like John B. Anderson of Illinois made some very powerful and persuasive arguments regarding this issue. Anderson said, "The costs of campaigns have become too high, the quality of campaign discourse too compromised, and public confidence in the legitimacy of the electoral process has ebbed too low to permit politics as usual to continue to govern our efforts in this area." Representative Donald W. Riegle Jr. of Michigan also expressed concern over the issue of campaign finance. Riegle, citing Congressman Paul N. McClosky Jr. of California, feared that "the vast influences of money in politics" were corrupting the political process. More important, Riegle emphasized a very powerful point that McClosky made: "we can never forget that we are a nation which operates by the consent of the governed. Our people must consent to file honest tax returns, consent to give honest judgment in jury cases, consent to serve in the armed services in time of conflict. That consent is and can only be based on faith in government—faith that government is honest and faith that it is truthful."

While I agreed with Anderson, Riegle, and McClosky, I still had some reservations about the campaign finance bill, H.R. 11060. Although I saw the campaign costs spiraling upwards, I had to consider my constituents when voting on any issue. In this instance, my friends in the radio and television industry in Mississippi were concerned over some of the bill's provisions. I received a telegram from Bob McRaney, senior executive secretary of the Mississippi Broadcasters Association, stating that small radio and TV stations in Mississippi were concerned because the bill required "the lowest unit rate in radio and TV" and in doing so discriminated "against small stations." McRaney added that the people he represented were asking for "fair and equitable treatment on access to facilities by candidates and that the limit of 10 cents per voter be applied to all media and eliminate the previous which limit[ed] electronic media to 6 cents a voter."

Bob was not the only one expressing these concerns. Robert F. Wright, president and general manager of WTOK-TV in Meridian, also articulated his fears "relative to the discriminatory manner in which the broadcast industry [was] treated in the Federal Elections Campaign Act of 1971." He argued, "From our standpoint, we do not make money on politics. As a matter of fact, in most instances, we lose money. Nevertheless, after a while, we do get tired of being a whipping dog whenever anyone has a beef.

I would appreciate it if you would use your influence to eliminate the discrimination from the Senate-House Bill."

Well, I took the concerns of McRaney and Wright and other considerations into account when I voted against the Federal Elections Campaign Act (FECA) of 1971. When the bill was amended and addressed the next year in H.R. 15267, however, I voted for the bill. So I have indeed had a hand in passing campaign finance reform.

Despite our best efforts in 1971 and 1972, campaign finance remained a concern throughout the remainder of the decade and well into the 1980s, and any victory in the curtailing of campaign spending was short lived. The political action committee, or PAC, sprouted almost immediately after FECA was passed. In the late 1960s and early 1970s there were about 90 corporate PACs. By 1984, the number of PACs had increased to 1,600. Another factor that contributed to the campaign finance crisis was "soft money" contributions from private citizens who might not necessarily be associated with a particular corporation or, for that matter, with a particular political party.

Throughout the 1980s FECA legislation was tinkered with and amended to address the ever-changing landscape of campaign finance. Did any of this legislation really succeed? Well, one need only look at recent elections and the campaign money raised to answer this question. To be fair, however, these problems with campaign financing are not owing to any lack of congressional action.

In 1998 Representatives Chris Shays, a Republican from Connecticut, and Marty Meehan, a Democrat from Massachusetts, pushed the House leadership to pass some sort of bipartisan campaign finance reform called the Shays-Meehan Bill. Three years later in the Senate the McCain-Feingold campaign finance bill was introduced by Senator John McCain of Arizona and Senator Russ Feingold of Wisconsin. This legislation was almost identical to the Shays-Meehan Bill. "That's right. It's almost the same bill," Feingold admitted in a CNN interview. "In fact," he added, "Congressman Shays and Congressman Meehan have gotten a similar bill through the House two times before." The Wisconsin senator then concluded, "Hopefully the Senate can accept this good piece of legislation and send it on to President Bush for his signature."

Senator McCain agreed with Feingold but was less optimistic about the passage of the campaign finance reform legislation. He said that the bill was good, and he thought the president would sign it. "But have no doubt," he added, "the big money and special interests that would lose their influence in Washington are doing everything they can to stop it at this point because they know that if it passes the House again that it's going to become law." McCain then said that restricting contributions would deprive special interests of "their influence," resulting in intensified "ferocity of the opposition" to block the legislation.

After a few more questions and answers, McCain ended the interview by reiterating the strength of the opposition to campaign finance reform. He said, "Look, those that use money to wield influence in Washington perceive this as a threat to their influence. And so they're going to do everything they can to just try to stop this bill. And so there is so much at stake that they'll be doing just about everything they can [to stop campaign finance reform legislation]."

The issue of campaign finance remains a hot topic on Capitol Hill. As of July 12, 2001, the Shays-Meehan Bill was derailed. As for the McCain-Feingold Bill, it too remains in a state of flux. But people must be patient. Considering all of the ideas and influences that factor into politics, it takes some time to make changes. Just read the chapter on my fight for a new GI bill as a case in point.

Nonetheless, someday Congress is going to have to take a hard look at this issue. I think we should emulate the British system of campaign financing. Under the Election and Referendums Act of 2000, all public donations for any candidate running for office in Britain must be made public. The impetus of this act is to insure that all gifts are above reproach and any suspicion that they influence policy. In our system, while there are limits placed on the candidate, they can still raise $100,000 or more in "anonymous" donations. This is indeed an issue that can be resolved. We all must be diligent in our efforts to reign in campaign financing lest we risk the integrity of our political system.

IX

The Flag Amendment

In the early 90s some of us in Congress were quite upset that some Americans were burning our great flag after the Supreme Court had ruled it was not illegal to do so. The only way this American flag burning could be stopped was to amend the United States Constitution, which took two-thirds votes in both houses, and ratification required that three-fourths of all the states approved. The House has passed a flag desecration act three times, but the Senate has not been able to get the two-thirds vote needed to pass it there.

I handled part of this resolution in the House in 1995. We got 98 Democrats and 219 Republicans to support the measure. I worked especially hard on my Democratic colleagues and did pretty well, getting almost a hundred votes. The statement that we wanted added as an amendment to the Constitution was simple and to the point: "The Congress and the States shall have power to prohibit the physical desecration of the flag of the United States."

On March 12, 1995, I spoke in the House on the amendment to stop desecration of the flag. I remarked that I strongly supported the legislation being presented by my New York friend Gerry Solomon, who chaired the Rules Committee. I continued, "As the chairman of the Committee on Rules mentioned, we have 242 members who have signed up on the House side to sponsor this." I said we needed 48 more Members to get up to 290 so that when we got the opportunity to bring this constitutional amendment resolution up, it would have a chance to pass. I thanked Congressman Gene Green of Texas, who had worked hard to get our fellow Democrats to sign on as cosponsors. I went on to point out: "As the gentleman from New York said, it is non-partisan. It comes about that we did pass a simple law in the Congress and signed by President Bush that said you cannot hurt this great American flag. This was turned down by the U.S. Supreme Court, who said Congress does not have that authority."

This decision forced us to change our strategy. I said in my March 21 remarks: "So it becomes now to protect the flag. We have all the veterans' organizations totally supporting this amendment. I stand right with the gentleman [Solomon], side by side. We need to get this constitutional amendment. We need to get more signees on this side of the Capitol to be darned sure. We lost some of them last time, as the gentleman remembers. We had over 290 signatures on the House side. When we brought the amendment up, we lost some, and we did not pass it. We do not want that to happen this time."

The debate was long and spirited. During the course of that

debate, Gerry Solomon presented for inclusion in the *Congres-sional Record* an article written by Congressman William Jeffer-son of Louisiana entitled "Flag Amendment Is the People's Will," which was published in the *American Legion Magazine*. The arti-cle was printed in the June 27, 1995, edition of the *Record*. I quote the article in its entirety here because it reflects my own views, plus Congressman Jefferson does a wonderful job of set-ting the flag amendment controversy in an historical perspective:

In April a proposed constitutional amendment that would per-mit the individual states to enact legislation banning physical desecration of the flag was introduced in the Congress.

After much careful deliberation, I became an original cospon-sor of the amendment. My decision came not without consider-able anguish, particularly over the principle of amending the Con-stitution.

In the final analysis, however, it came down to this: If we are not willing to stand up for our flag, what will we stand up for?

To those who say this is a First Amendment issue—an issue of free speech—let me remind them that there are several restric-tions and limits on speech already. One cannot libel or slander another without fear of legal retribution. One cannot advocate the assassination of the President without the Secret Service becoming extremely interested in his or her speech. As Supreme Court Justice Felix Frankfurter pointed out so eloquently, many years ago, our right to free speech does not extend to yelling "Fire!" in a crowded theater. No, this is not a free speech issue. Rather, it is a matter of personal accountability.

Surely, desecrating a U.S. Flag—burning a flag—is abhorred by society, and our society has the right to demand that such activity be punished. Reflecting that sentiment, my home state of Louisiana in 1991 was the 21st of 49 states so far to pass a resolution urging Congress to approve a flag-protection amendment.

Amending the Constitution is no simple undertaking. The Founding Fathers intended it to be that way. Two-thirds of the House (290 members) and Senate (67) must agree to pass the legislation, then three-fourths of the states—36—must ratify the amendment within seven years.

Throughout our history, constitutional amendments have proved the only path for redress of serious societal ills in our country. Women's suffrage, for example, was accomplished through a constitutional amendment, as was the abolition of slavery after the Civil War. The Fourteenth Amendment recognized former slaves as citizens and the Fifteenth gave them the right to vote. No one could deny that these amendments—controversial as they were at the time—made our society better.

This proposed amendment and the need of its passage grew from a 1989 Supreme Court decision, Texas v. Johnston. The court narrowly ruled, 5-4, that burning an American flag was "protected" as free speech. The case arose following a demonstration at the Republican National Convention in Dallas in 1984.

Gregory Johnson and a group of fellow protesters burned a flag outside the convention hall as part of their protest. Texas authorities convicted Johnston of flag desecration under existing Texas law. The Supreme Court decision overturned not only the Texas law but also flag-protection statutes in 47 other states and the District of Columbia.

The American public was outraged then and continues to be outraged today. Public-opinion polls show that more than 80 percent of all Americans favor protection of the flag. Following the 1989 Supreme Court decision and a similar 5-4 decision in 1990 in another flag desecration case, three out of four Americans believed the only way to protect the flag was through a constitutional amendment.

Nearly forty years ago in the hot summer of 1957, Dr. Martin Luther King was beginning his dream of equality for all Americans. At a citizenship education program that summer, King said there was glory in citizenship, and that we don't want haters. Our country, he said, may not be all we want it to be, but that would change.

Respect your country; honor its flag.

We have come a long way as a nation since 1957. Dr. King's dream still lives—the American dream persists. In the words of Charles Evan Hughes, the 11th Chief Justice of the U.S. Supreme Court, "This flag means more than association and reward. It is the symbol of our national unity."

It is now time to do our patriotic duty, to keep faith with the

American people who sent us to Washington. Passing this flag-protection amendment adds one more strand to the fabric woven by preceding generations—the fabric of freedom, symbolized by our flag.

I still find Congressman Jefferson's ringing defense of our flag very moving, and I still endorse, without any reservation, his patriotic comments. I find it hard even now to fathom how some people, including many of my well-meaning colleagues in the House at the time, can equate free speech with flag burning. Burning a flag is a physical act, not an exercise in verbalizing.

I ran across Supreme Court Justice Scalia right after the Supreme Court had struck down the law that burning the flag was illegal. I had written Justice Scalia a letter earlier stating my disappointment. When I saw him at the Army-Navy Country Club tennis courts, I asked him if he had gotten my letter, and he smiled and said he had. That was the end of the conversation. I like Justice Scalia but think he was wrong on the flag-burning decision. I confess that even now I cannot grasp how the majority of the learned members of the court could see the prevention of flag burning as a threat to free speech.

During the debate over the issue, my friend Charles Canady, congressman from Florida, made some strong arguments in favor of preventing flag desecration, and I thought he did a great job in quoting comments of Supreme Court justices, past and present (as of the mid-90s), that supported his position. He quoted Justice John Paul Stevens, who said of the flag, "It is a symbol of freedom, of equal opportunity, of religious tolerance, and of good will for other peoples who share our aspirations." And he noted that Justice Hugo Black once said, "It passes my belief that anything in the Federal Constitution bars a state from making the deliberate burning of the American flag an offense." Further, he cited Justice William Rehnquist's words that the desecration of the flag "is most likely to be indulged in not to express any particular idea, but to antagonize others." Canady said strongly in his House remarks: "The Solomon-Montgomery amendment will overturn the opinions of the Supreme Court in Johnson and Eichman [a previous case in which the Court ruled against flag protection] by restoring the authority to Congress and the States to prohibit the physical desecration of the flag."

Of course during the debate I spoke many times myself in defense of my position. Though I always respected the rights of my colleagues to disagree with me or anybody else on any issue, I still found it strange that so many were willing to ignore facts. On June 28, 1995, I said during the floor debate, "Mr. Speaker, we need to set the record straight. They are saying that flags had not been burned around the country, and they are going back to 1994. Only two blocks from here, Mr. Speaker, they burned two flags on June 14. A fellow had a nice cake down there and was passing out the cake, and two nuts came up and started burning the

American flag. The Interior Department tried to stop them. So, we need this bill. They are burning the flags only two blocks from here."

That same day, I spoke again, elaborating on more points raised by anti-flag amendment House members. Sometimes it is difficult to be diplomatic when you feel as strongly about an issue as I do about protecting our flag. Yet, as House members, we all tried to remember that we represented the people from our districts and that they expected us to respect each other. I always tried to do that, and I think my remarks reflect that. I arose and said, "I think that this debate has been good for all of us. We are all learning more about the Constitution, and that is what it is all about. I was reading opinions from constitutional scholars, Steven Presser of Northwestern University among them, and they keep coming back to the idea that blowing up buildings, doing crazy things on the streets, is really not an expression of freedom and goes beyond common sense. Therefore, burning the flag is beyond common sense and, therefore, the flag amendment does not hurt the first amendment freedom of speech. I think that is a very, very strong point, that when you are burning the flag, you are going beyond the common speech or the common sense that individuals are entitled to in this country. Mr. Speaker, there are more signatures—and I have been around here quite a while—that is the most signatures I have ever seen from the American people, over 1 million signatures saying that they want a constitutional amendment. I want to commend the American Legion and other veterans' organizations, plus the Citizen Flag Alliance, for going out and getting signatures. This is what the people want, Mr. Speaker. They want a constitutional amendment; over 80 percent of them in a poll have said that. We ought to give them what they want."

Again, later in the debate that same day, I elaborated on other key aspects. "I have made the point several times over the past few weeks that this is a bipartisan effort. This is not Democrat or Republican. It is a matter of protecting the single most recognized symbol of freedom and democracy in the world. We tried in 1990 to simply pass a law to protect the flag. Most of us voted for it. But the Supreme Court ruled it unconstitutional. That means the only way that we can achieve this goal is by a constitutional amendment. This amendment will not infringe on anyone's first amendment rights. We are the most tolerant country on Earth when it comes to dissent and criticism of our Government. But I really draw the line on the physical desecration of this great flag. I think the American people agree. In fact, the gentleman from New York [Gerry Solomon] has a folder that shows 49 of our States have passed resolutions in support of our efforts."

I then turned to a discussion of how I thought many young people were viewing the debate. I continued, "Each session of the House of Representatives, when we are opening session, we start off, as you know, Mr. Speaker, with a prayer and the Pledge of Allegiance. Every time we have a group of students that are in the gallery from elementary school on up, they proudly join in, and you will see it this week. They will join in. You will hear their young voices ring out: I pledge allegiance to the flag of the United States of America. They know the pledge, and they know what the flag means to our country. They do not understand why anyone should be allowed to desecrate the flag. Mr. Speaker, neither do I."

I then concluded this portion of my address by zeroing in on patriotic implications of the debate. "The flag has rallied our troops in battle," I said, "and it has brought us together in times of national tragedy because it holds such an emotional place in our lives. And I am emotional, too. It is worthy of the protection we seek in this legislation. Now, our Founding Fathers never dreamed someone would desecrate the flag. If they had, the protections would have been written into the Constitution 219 years ago. Mr. Speaker, over a million Americans have died in defense of this flag. We owe it to them to adopt this amendment. God bless our great country."

I would like to include here, too, some excerpts from a truly special piece written by Mike O'Callaghan, former governor of Nevada and executive editor of the *Las Vegas Sun* at the time he wrote about Flag Day. The article, entitled "Fly and Protect Old Glory," was included in the *Congressional Record* during the debate over protecting the flag. In addressing the debate he said, "There is nothing wrong with disagreeing with any attempt to amend the document which spells out the strengths of our nation. The Constitution was written so it can be amended from time to time. Before it is amended, there should be long discussions about the content of any amendment before it is approved by Congress and/or the state legislatures. Those who argue against this latest suggested amendment are no less patriotic than are those who believe the amendment is a necessity." O'Callaghan went on to point out that the actions of the Supreme Court, by declaring flag-protection laws unconstitutional, had forced flag supporters to seek redress via a constitutional amendment.

He then discussed the opposing sides. "The American Legion," he wrote, "has taken the forefront in pushing for a ban on flag desecration. The American Civil Liberties Union has taken the opposite point of view because that organization views such an amendment as weakening the First Amendment's protection of free speech." He noted that the Clinton administration had embraced the ACLU's position as had liberals like Ted Kennedy and liberal newspapers like the *Los Angeles Times*. O'Callaghan then stated firmly, "I find it necessary to disagree with the ACLU, the Clinton administration, Sen. Kennedy and the *Los Angeles Times*. This won't be the first or last time that I have or will disagree with this distinguished group of intellectuals. . . . The entire amending process is a series of political actions provided for by the instrument being amended. As I have written before, I'm more than a little insulted by the inane argument that such a constitutional change will be an infringement on our right of free speech. That argument, made by many who oppose an amendment to protect the flag, has little or nothing to do with damaging the First Amendment. A person can write and talk all day long and into the night about the shortcomings of our city, state, and nation. That same person, if angry enough, can renounce his or her citizenship without being worried about being jailed. Millions of Americans believe public desecration of our nation's symbol is taking it one step beyond acceptable behavior and is an act beyond the bounds of free speech."

O'Callaghan then quoted a Navajo friend of his who had watched our flag being unfurled on Mount Surabachi after the Battle of Iwo Jima: "Passage of this amendment is but one small step toward restoring some accountability for one's actions. Responsibility for one's actions is part of being a citizen of this country."

I suppose that is a part of the issue that disturbs me a great deal. Too many well-meaning people seem to think it is dangerous to be patriotic, to be a practitioner of citizenship in the sense of standing by our country, no matter what kind of complaints we may have. With a nation as large as ours, there are bound to be people unhappy with the government from time to time. There is no way everyone is going to be pleased about everything. On the other hand, if all of us embraced anarchy, and did whatever pleased us, when it pleased us, our country would fall apart quickly. It just seems to me that there are some basics that we as Americans must adhere to if we are to remain a free people. Tolerance is fine, and, as I have said, we, as a nation, are probably the most tolerant people on earth. But if we wreck the symbols and values that hold us together, what do we have left? I would argue, not very much that is worthwhile.

I think of the images we have seen recently of how America has come together in the wake of our being assaulted by terrorists. The one symbol, the one object that has been displayed, waved, worn on clothes, and attached to vehicle windows is the American flag. So many people have rushed to find flags that there was actually a shortage for a time. Does that not tell us how important the flag is to our country, to our citizens? I truly hope that one day we can get beyond spurious arguments, however well intentioned, and do what seems to me, and I believe to millions and millions of my fellow Americans, a simple obvious thing—legally protect our flag from desecration. Getting three-fourths of the states to ratify would be no problem, in my opinion. As noted above, forty-nine states have already passed resolutions supporting an amendment to the Constitution making it illegal to burn our flag.

Many thousands of people have died in combat and elsewhere fighting for and defending our flag. I suspect that, given the state of the world, many more of our friends, neighbors, and family members will be asked to make the ultimate sacrifice. We have to have a symbol that means something to all of us, and the flag stands for our country's greatness. I fought as hard as I could in the House when I was there to stop the desecration, but we just could never win in the Senate. I pray that the issue does not go away. The top priority for the American Legion (our largest veterans' organization) is to pass the flag amendment. They are not going to give up and will continue to fight yearly until they achieve victory. I trust that likewise we as a people will not give up. The flag itself is merely a piece of cloth, but what it stands for and the price so many have paid to defend it are priceless. To prevent its desecration is at once the least and the best that we can do.

X

House Prayer Breakfast

U pon my arrival to the United States Congress in January of 1967, a fellow congressman informed me that several House members participated in a prayer breakfast every Thursday morning from 8 to 9 A.M. in one of the House dining rooms on Capitol Hill. Interested, I at once became actively involved with the House Prayer Breakfast group.

Throughout my life I have attended church, and I believe in the Bible and in Jesus Christ and His teachings. I was and still am an Episcopalian, and I know the service and rituals of the Episcopal Church. I must confess, however, that I am not a student of the Bible and that there are many religious mysteries that I hope will be answered in my lifetime. In my Prayer Book there are several verses that inspire, guide, and help me to be a better person. God, I believe, listens to and answers most of my prayers. He has guided me through many areas of life—the joys and the pitfalls—and given me strength, success, and good health.

It was this devotion to God and the teachings of Jesus Christ that enabled me to join my fellow congressmen in sharing in the fellowship of our weekly prayer breakfasts. I have many fond memories of these gatherings and especially remember the first few times I attended the breakfasts in 1967. During this time there were only about eight of us in attendance: Chaplain Latch and six or seven House members, including myself. We all got along splendidly and shared stories of work, family, and life in general. But as the years passed, more became involved, and when I left the House some thirty to forty members attended the weekly meetings. More important, the prayer breakfast is only exclusive to House members, former members, and invited guests. Religious affiliation and political alliances are not prerequisites for membership.

The diversity of membership is best exemplified in the group's three officers: the president (who presides over the meeting), the vice president, and the secretary. Each congressional session we rotate; if the president is a Democrat, then the vice president is a Republican and the secretary is either a Democrat or a Republican. To participate as an officer, one must start as secretary and work up to the position of president. Each week a Democrat or Republican leads our discussion; selecting speakers is the responsibility of the officers.

Each meeting is similar to a church service. We have a scripture reading, and then a report is read regarding members and their families concerning sickness, deaths, weddings, and births. The members then sing a song. I must admit that we are no choirboys and that no record company is beating down our door for a recording contract, but I think it is good for visitors and staff to hear Christian songs resonating from the Nation's capital.

Following the song, a selected member talks for a few minutes. These discussions have an inspirational theme, and each individual takes away something valuable from the speaker's experience. The discussion leader talks for about ten minutes and then fields questions and comments from the attendees.

I have been very active in the House Prayer Breakfast. On the occasions I was president, for example, I influenced the actual programs. At a July 1970 program, I had my distinguished colleague Congressman Daniel Flood of Pennsylvania to speak on the "Doldrums and Storms" found in everyday life. I shared these remarks with the other members of the House. In his talk, Flood discussed the "doldrums." The doldrums begin when all is calm, he explained, and build into a storm like a hurricane. But the doldrums can cause a storm among humanity, too. Think of Germany prior to World War II, "defeated, humiliated, ground into the dust . . . in disgrace and in debt, into just these doldrums . . . Hitler came and stirred up such a storm as the world had never seen before." A powerful point, but more significantly, my fellow congressman said that America was in the doldrums—a spiritual doldrums. Weaving spirituality into his discourse, Flood said the country could change "the climate . . . by the power of faith . . . our prayer here today is for our Country and for our world." These were most inspirational words, and at each breakfast I could count on such words and fellowship to lift my spirits and carry me through my busy week.

On May 15, 2000, Congressman Ed Pease of Indiana along with my fellow Mississippians Chip Pickering and Roger Wicker introduced H.R. 491. The statement read as follows: "Whereas former Representative G. V. 'Sonny' Montgomery of Mississippi, from the time of his election to the House of Representatives in 1967 and . . . beyond his retirement in 1996 through the present day, has faithfully and continuously facilitated the 'House of Representatives Prayer Breakfast' at 8 A.M. every Thursday morning in Room H-130 in the House of Representatives." For this service, which is "indelibly etched in the memories of the many Members who have attended" these breakfasts, the House honored me by changing the name of the room. Through Congress committees, approval of the Senate, and signature of the president most legislation is passed. In this instance, however, the Resolution was introduced to the full House and was passed by a voice vote. But there was still some politics involved in passing this resolution. I told Ed Pease and Congressman Bob Stump of Arizona that I did not want a roll call vote because some might vote against the idea of naming a room in the Capitol. I should add here that any vote against renaming room H-130 after me was not necessarily against me but against the entire concept of renaming any room in the building. Yet, despite my discussion with Congressmen Stump and Pease, someone did call for a vote on May 15, 2000, and it passed 380–0. Since there are some days in the House when the Ten Commandments might get a few opposing votes, I was indeed pleased by this outcome.

On the day of the dedication, many congressmen and other important people in Washington were in attendance: Congressman Zach Wamp of Tennessee, president of the House Prayer Breakfast; Reverend James Ford, chaplain emeritus of the U.S. House of Representatives; Congressman Ray LaHood of Illinois, secretary of the House Prayer Breakfast; Congressman Richard Gephardt of Missouri, Democratic leader of the House; Congressman Bart Stupak Sr. of Michigan; and Reverend Daniel Coughlin, current chaplain of the House. I was deeply honored and touched to have such a distinguished group of people at the dedication.

Many kind words were said on my behalf at the dedication. Congressman Wamp made the most memorable remarks. Wamp and I, along with other well-known politicians such as Governor Carroll Campbell and Senators Bill Brock and Howard Baker, as well as business leader and media mogul Ted Turner, attended the McCallie Military School in Chattanooga, Tennessee. I am often embarrassed when people praise me for what I see as just doing what is right. The same could be said in this instance regarding the kind words of my fellow congressman and military school alumnus. Congressman Wamp began his speech with a little background of the House Prayer Breakfast. He then expressed my feelings about our weekly meetings, stating: "[Sonny] comes every week. Thursday morning, folks, for an hour is a sacrosanct set-aside time." How true. As I mentioned earlier, the fellowship and spirituality that I experience at the weekly breakfasts is very important to me; it gives me strength to carry out my weekly tasks and obligations. Congressman Wamp said, "This is a special hour for Members to come in a non-denominational, interfaith way, and just share our faith in God and understand the goodness in each of us and . . . share with each other in a human way so that in the middle of what people see as a war here sometimes on Capitol Hill, there is peace and tranquility as we all share in our humanness together." I could not have said it better.

Congressman Wamp continued, "Every week 'Sonny' is there, year in, year out, decade in, decade out, he is the rock, the anchor. And H-130 where we meet in that sacrosanct fellowship every week should be named after him in his honor." He then closed: "There is no more love in this institution than the love for 'Sonny' Montgomery." These were not, however, the only kind words uttered that day. Congressman Pease, the one who introduced the legislation to rename H-130, said, "Thursday morning with 'Sonny' and our other colleagues provides an oasis for the spirit, an understanding that each of us is a very small part on a continuum of history of a great nation."

So the room name was changed in honor of me, the "zealous guardian of this one hour per week," as my fellow congressman and Mississippian Rodger Wicker had once said. I may have left my "imprint all over the Third District of Mississippi," as my replacement and fellow Mississippian Chip Pickering has said, but I have also left my mark in Washington, D.C.

The dedication ceremony began at 4:30 P.M. and lasted until 5:15 P.M. After the dedication, there was a reception in the House Veterans' Affairs Committee room in the Cannon Office Building. This reception, however, served a dual purpose. We gathered to celebrate the naming of the room as well as my eightieth birthday on August 5. I have had some big birthday parties during my eighty years, but this one proved to be the largest I ever had; 250 people stopped by to say hello and wish me a happy birthday.

The sheer size of the party would have satisfied me for a lifetime, but I also received some wonderful gifts. Probably the biggest and most expensive present was a crystal replica of the United States Capitol. This gift along with all the flowers and cards from around the nation made the day extra special. Thanks to the work done by my business associate, Greg Sharp, president of the Spectrum Group, and his associate Medora Wilson, and Louise Medlin, vice president of the Montgomery Group, I had a terrific birthday celebration. It is my sincere hope that I have a few more birthdays left in me, but none will be as wonderful as my eightieth.

As you can probably tell, I am a spiritual and dedicated person. The House Prayer Breakfast serves as an outlet for these characteristics. But while spirituality is important on Capitol Hill, it is also significant to our nation. As you will recall, Congressman Flood of Pennsylvania said in 1971 that we needed to pray for our country's well being to get out of what he termed the spiritual "doldrums." In other words, we as leaders have a responsibility to bring the word of God to the people. For this reason, I also became involved with the National Prayer Breakfast.

The National Prayer Breakfast began in 1952. On February 3, 1952, preacher Billy Graham gave a speech on the east steps of the Capitol. In this speech Rev. Graham suggested that the Congress call on President Harry S. Truman to set aside a day in which members of all religious faiths could spend in meditation and prayer. Truman agreed with the idea and requested that Congress pass an appropriate resolution to create a day of national prayer. My predecessors wasted little time in answering the call. On February 27, 1952, House Joint Resolution 382 "to provide for setting aside an appropriate day as a National Day of Prayer" was introduced to the House. The clerk then read the joint resolution as follows: "That the President shall set aside and proclaim a suitable day each year, other than a Sunday, as a National Day of Prayer, on which the people of the United States may turn to God in prayer and meditation and churches, in groups, and as individuals." After three readings of the resolution, it was passed.

In 1953 the first annual Presidential Prayer Breakfast was organized during President Dwight Eisenhower's first term. In attendance were some of America's most powerful evangelical preachers and political leaders. By 1954, the breakfast had really taken hold as President Dwight Eisenhower, Vice President Richard Nixon, several cabinet members, and congressmen attended the special event. Chief Justice Earl Warren was one of the speakers. The breakfast closed with the six hundred guests singing President Eisenhower's favorite hymn, "What a Friend We Have in Jesus." I should tell you that Eisenhower never liked "Presidential" attached to the prayer breakfast, so he dropped it and the name became the National Prayer Breakfast.

During my thirty years of congressional service I never missed a National Prayer Breakfast. The occasion is held once a year in Washington's largest hotel, the Washington Hilton. It is this one day of national prayer that brings together each president and vice president in office, most of the cabinet members, and half the Senate and House members. The House and Senate Breakfast leaders take the leadership role during alternate years.

I attended my first National Prayer Breakfast as a freshman congressman on October 18, 1967. Four short years later I greeted the breakfast group on behalf of the House. On February 10, 1971, my mother was in attendance and seated beside Rev. Billy Graham. It was an exciting day as I addressed the distinguished crowd.

I began my introduction with the traditional "Good morning, Mr. President, Mrs. Nixon, my colleagues in the Government, and guests of the 1971 National Prayer Breakfast." I also took the opportunity to remind all in attendance about the House Breakfast Group and how we met every Thursday morning and that the gatherings were casual, informal, and nondenominational. To offer further insight into the meetings, I informed the audience that the remarks made at the Thursday meetings were "excellent . . . thought-provoking and soul-searching, some amusing, some sad, but all sincere. Topics range from personal testimonies to politics and religion to the subject that prayer and religion bring men together mentally and physically." I then hit upon the benefits of these House Prayer Breakfasts. As I have already relayed, it is the camaraderie and fellowship among my fellow congressmen that is most important to me. This is the message I relayed to the National Breakfast Group when I said: "I have a great feeling of personal renewal, because I have been provided an opportunity of fellowship with my colleagues that would not be possible in any other situation, especially on the House floor during some of our heated debates."

Another benefit of the House Prayer Breakfasts was that they made us better people for having been there. I said, "We who attend the prayer group know we are better congressmen and -women and individuals because of the meetings." To support this assertion, I noted that fellow Congressman Dan Kuykendall of Tennessee often remarked that "the prayer breakfast is the only meeting in Washington he does not mind arriving 15 minutes early and staying late."

I concluded my remarks with a humorous story, telling President Nixon and the crowd, "We have some good laughs at our meetings, and in fact the prayer group is my best source of jokes, Mr. President, suitable for telling at home." I then relayed a joke that I had heard from Congressman Wilmer Mizell of North Carolina regarding his church during one of its regular meetings. "The Board of Deacons had recommended that the church buy a chandelier," I began. "Everyone was in agreement but one man who stood up and said he was against buying a chandelier for three reasons. First, no one could spell the word. Secondly, no one could play it. And thirdly, what the church needed was more light." As the crowd chuckled I said, "There is a brighter light on Capitol Hill today because of our weekly prayer breakfast meetings."

Immediately following my introductory remarks, the Honorable John H. Wheeler, president of Mechanics and Farmers Bank, read from Isaiah 1:10–20 (which emphasizes worshiping together for the betterment of mankind). Other speakers included Republican Senator Clifford Hansen of Wyoming, a member of the Senate Prayer Breakfast Group, and Speaker of the House and Oklahoman, the Honorable Carl Albert. The latter in particular offered some thought-provoking remarks as he led us in the Prayer for National Leaders. Albert said, "We turn to Thee with a petition for Thy involvement with our nation's leaders—men with honored responsibilities in the judicial, legislative, and executive areas." He then ended his prayer: "Help us to be a part of Thy answer to this petition." These were very powerful words that have remained with me ever since.

Another memorable National Prayer Breakfast was in February of 1984. The invitations are sent during October and November prior to the New Year. By this time I had become a regular at this annual event and was involved in creating the guest list. As committee member William L. Armstrong emphasized, the guests "represent a cross section of our national life." For this particular Prayer Breakfast I chose Dr. and Mrs. Otis Seal from my hometown of Meridian to be my guests. At the time, Dr. Seal was serving as a pastor of Calvary Baptist Church. I felt, because of his service to his parish and the community, he represented what was good about religion in the Magnolia State.

My friend and then vice president George Bush said the opening prayer. The Seals and I sat and listened contentedly to each speaker. I remember, too, that when President Ronald Reagan spoke, he emphasized the theme that had been relayed to me in the October and November memos: a cross section of society being represented at the breakfast. But President Reagan took it one step further when he mentioned other religions from around the world. He told of how an Asian monk living in the fourth century used the power of prayer to stop the violent gladiator battles in the Roman Colosseum. It was not only an inspiring tale but an educational one as well.

The 1984 National Prayer Breakfast was all that I expected: inspirational, educational, and relaxing. I was especially pleased that my two guests, Otis and Jacque Seal, were in attendance and enjoyed the experience. Shortly after the breakfast, Dr. Seal wrote me a kind letter. He said, "Words are inadequate to express to you my sincere appreciation for the privilege, honor, and opportunity of sitting with you at the President's Prayer Breakfast. My wife Jacque joins me in saying thank you with all our hearts. It was the most blessed and memorable occasion ever in our life." Dr.

Seal also mentioned that he learned much about Washington while he was there and thanked my assistants Beverly Buckley and Laurie Hall "for being patient and helping a Mississippi country boy understand many things that go on in our nation's capital." I was especially heartened by the reverend's closing remarks: "You and your staff will be in my prayers more often than before. Those of us who are holding the torch here will try to keep it burning and pass it on so that future generations may have the joy of living in this God blessed America."

Dr. and Mrs. Seal were among the many folks I have helped obtain invitations to the National Prayer Breakfast throughout the years. As their account of the 1984 gala can attest, the many foreign dignitaries—presidents and prime ministers alike—make the breakfast a wonderful event. And, unlike the singing at the House Prayer Breakfasts, there are singing groups brought from different parts of the country to perform various kinds of gospel music.

Each National Prayer Breakfast is energizing and exciting. The president of the United States always attends and talks on a religious subject. Most recently, in the year 2000, President Bill Clinton was there as well as many international leaders. I hosted table 2, which seated ten people. Among this group were three presidents and their wives from the Pacific Islands region. Connecticut Senator Joe Lieberman opened the event. He began by talking about this tradition's great history. "I want to begin by talking with you about the weekly Senate Prayer Breakfasts—

those still-small gatherings that have, along with their counterpart in the House, spawned this magnificent National Prayer Breakfast as well as similar meetings in every American state and so many countries around the world." Lieberman's words were perfect. He incorporated what the breakfast was and had become over almost half a century.

Lieberman also discussed spirituality and how it could strengthen the nation—yet another aspect of the National Prayer Breakfasts. "Let me suggest that we begin by talking more to each other about our beliefs and our values, talking in the spirit of this prayer breakfast—open, generous, and mutually respectful—so that we may strengthen each other in our common quest." This is the fellowship that I have talked so much about. If we work together and gain an understanding of one another, then, as a nation, we can move forward spiritually.

These prayer breakfasts, House, Senate, and National, are good for the country. All of them illustrate that the American people are God-fearing; these people do go to God for guidance and help when they are troubled and confused. I, too, will add that I have never met an atheist in Congress. While some members have different religious beliefs than mine, we share a common belief in an almighty God. This faith is the bond between all of us. There are many crises in Washington, be they political or personal, and many have involved congressional members at some time or another. I can assure you that God's assistance in the government of this country is often sought by those who serve in Congress, this writer included.

But the impact of the Prayer Breakfasts, especially the National Prayer Breakfast, goes beyond the United States borders. I have received letters from many foreign leaders and dignitaries that convey the same sense of spiritual unity that I have felt after attending one of these events. In 1975, for example, Dr. William R. Tolbert Jr., former president of Liberia, sent a note expressing his gratitude for the "great privilege and honor" of attending the Twenty-third Annual National Prayer Breakfast. He said that the event was "spiritually uplifting" and that he hoped "mankind everywhere [would] hasten the removal of all barriers to universal progress and prosperity, the breaking of every wall that separates man from man and the building of all bridges that are needed to unite all individuals in one loving strong human family."

Dai Soon Lee, floor leader of the Democratic Justice Party in the National Assembly of the Republic of Korea, expressed similar feelings of joy and hope after attending the 1987 National Prayer Breakfast. He said that he appreciated the group's "sharing with me your prayers for my people and country and for the encouragement you have given me in spreading the Good Word and in promoting the Christian cause in Korea." He also mentioned that he faced an uphill battle in Korea's democratization, but as God wished he would try to devote his efforts in performing his tasks with "integrity and diligence." I could identify with these feelings because there have been many times that I have asked for God's help when making difficult decisions regarding the direction our nation should take.

As you can see, being involved in politics is more than just introducing, debating, and passing laws. It is an awesome responsibility to serve as a lawmaker and guide the nation in a forward direction. But being involved in the prayer breakfasts has afforded me the spiritual guidance and strength to cope with the stresses that not only come with the job as a United States congressman but with the stresses of life—the ups and downs—that we all experience. I could not have gotten this far in my career or my life had it not been for the Lord's guidance.

These sentiments are best summarized in a letter that I sent to colleagues as outgoing president of the House Prayer Breakfasts in April of 1971. I said, "My association with the [House] Prayer Breakfast group has enriched my spiritual life, inspired my feeling of duty to God and country, and generated meaningful friendships." Although I was addressing the House Prayer Breakfast group specifically, these words apply to the National Prayer Breakfasts as well.

XI

My Friendship with Senator John C. Stennis

As you already know by now, I attended Mississippi State University, which was Mississippi State College back then, from August 1939 through January 1943. But even before I arrived on campus I had heard of the legendary Judge John C. Stennis. He had graduated from State and then went on to the University of Virginia, where he earned his law degree. Stennis lived right up the road from Meridian in DeKalb, Kemper County. While I attended State, Stennis was serving as circuit judge and alumni association president. As alumni president, Stennis was on campus a great deal while I was at State. During my senior year (1942–43) I served as student body president. This is when I really got to know John C. Stennis, and we quickly became good friends. He was a very impressive person who dressed very well, always wearing a hamburg and a coat and tie. He was also a gifted speaker and a colorful person; all of us on campus tried to emulate the judge.

In January 1943, I marched off to fight the Nazi regime in Europe and was away from Mississippi for three years. When I came home in 1946 I was surprised to find out that Judge Stennis was running for the United States Senate. The opportunity to run for the seat came when longtime senator and former governor Theodore Bilbo died. The majority of Mississippi State alumni that I knew throughout the state supported Stennis. I was very excited that my friend was running for the Senate and quickly became involved in Judge Stennis's campaign. I worked out of Lauderdale County and with State graduates from around the state.

We worked very hard for Stennis, and our efforts paid off. Stennis defeated Congressman Bill Colmer from the Mississippi Gulf Coast in the second primary. As I recall, there was no Republican primary, and I have forgotten the name of the Republican who ran against Stennis. Interestingly enough, Bill Colmer approached me some twenty years later and told me he knew I worked against him when he ran in the Democratic primary against Stennis. Colmer even found some literature I had left in a car he borrowed from a dealer who had lent cars to candidates. But there were no hard feelings between us. After all, politics is politics, and you handle victory and defeat gracefully. Colmer was a wonderful man, always nice and helpful to me in Congress.

Stennis won the senate seat in 1947, and, as the old saying goes, "the rest is history." Working for Senator Stennis gave me a real taste for politics. I found that I liked the political arena and was proud of Senator Stennis for being our highest government official who graduated from Mississippi State. And, as I mentioned in my chapter on my early life, I worked with Stennis throughout my career as both a state senator and United States congressman. The senator and I had built on our friendship from the time I had met him as student body president at MSU and while we both served in office. Our bond was strong not just because we both bled maroon and white but because we both worked for and represented the people of Mississippi.

While in Washington I also became better acquainted with the senator's family. I enjoyed associating with Ms. Coy, his wife, and their two children, Margaret Jane and John Hampton. When the occasion arose that Mrs. Stennis and the children were in Washington, we had a few parties sponsored by the Mississippi Society. At these particular parties, the entire Mississippi delegation and families attended. We all had a grand time.

I was proud to be a close friend of Senator John C. Stennis. Sometimes you take it for granted that someone will always be a presence in your life and that nothing will interrupt the relationship. And then you have a scare and are brought back to the realization that life has its twists and turns and you had better appreciate and cherish your friendships. Well, there was a scare that certainly made me, the entire state of Mississippi, both houses of Congress, and the nation appreciate Senator Stennis even more.

On January 30, 1973, Senator Stennis was shot in front of his Washington, D.C., house by robbers. According to published reports, two men stole the senator's five-hundred-dollar pocket watch, the Phi Beta Kappa chain attached to the watch, and even the three dimes and nickel that were in his pocket. Ms. Coy, who was already in the house, said she heard "two pops" just before the senator came stumbling in and said he had been shot with a pistol. One bullet had entered his chest just below the left nipple, passed near but missed his heart and lung and lodged in his back. The other bullet struck his left leg and disintegrated. He was rushed to Walter Reed Hospital, where he underwent several hours of surgery. A delegation of senators and congressmen, myself included, went over to the hospital and waited. According to Democratic Senator Lloyd Bentsen from Texas, the prognosis was not good. Bentsen had spoken with Ms. Coy at the hospital, and after this visit, he told the delegation and reporters, "It's serious. It's very serious. It really is." Senator Bentsen was correct. We nearly lost him that night. Fortunately, however, there were some great doctors who had just returned from Vietnam and had treated thousands of serious gunshot wounds, and they worked on the Senator and saved his life.

There was an outpouring of compassion and concern as the nation awaited the senator's recovery. In both the House and the Senate, politicians not only expressed their concern over the senator's recovery but also showed how much Senator Stennis meant to them and the nation. Delegate Walter E. Fauntroy of the District of Columbia said, "The shooting of Senator Stennis is both a local and national tragedy." He also said, "If this [shooting] can happen to a man of such value, such integrity to our Nation and our city, it speaks important words to us wherever we are and in whatever station in life we hold." Fauntroy then added that this tragedy spoke to the nation's need to redouble its efforts to "bring economic and personal security to our troubled city, our troubled Nation, our troubled people."

I agreed with Delegate Fauntroy, especially his comments regarding personal safety in the D.C. area. The laws in Washington, D.C., were not very good when it came to protecting its citizens. On March 22, 1973, I spoke on the House floor about this issue, saying, "Mr. Speaker, the need for speedy consideration of President Nixon's crime proposals was pointed up this past weekend when the U.S. magistrate handling the hearing for the alleged attackers of Senator John Stennis greatly reduced the amount of bail being requested by the U.S. Attorney's office. I was greatly shocked to learn that one of the suspects had been released on an unsecured bond of $5,000 and another had the amount of bail reduced from $25,000 to $10,000."

The reason this reduction in bail was so distressing, I explained, was that in the case of Senator Stennis we were not talking about a simple "assault or mugging." Instead, this case involved "suspects in an armed robbery and attempted murder case, plus an assault on a Federal official." So, I felt that the president's anti-crime proposals would "end this leniency on the part of some courts that appear to take more interest in protecting the criminal than they do the rights of the victims of crime." The laws may not have been very good in Washington, D.C., prior to

Senator Stennis's harrowing experience, but, because of vigilance on the part of myself and other lawmakers, they were strengthened after he was hurt.

Fortunately, Senator Stennis made a full recovery from his gunshot wounds. By early February he was able to sit up, and all his vital signs were good. He was back in his office that summer. Stennis was also able to have some closure with his near fatal altercation. It seemed that the Senator never missed a beat. He and I attended a reception for the Oktibbeha County Historical and Genealogical Society at MSU in late October 1973. Stennis was his usual jovial and outgoing self, and it made me happy to see my friend pull his life back together in the face of such adversity.

It was also in October of 1973 that the Senator stood in front of the district court assemblage and identified his assailant—then nineteen-year-old Tyrone I. Marshall. Stennis not only identified Marshall but recalled the incident in great detail. He testified that even after Marshall had pulled the gun on him, he said, "I never gave up trying to persuade him, to argue, to negotiate the situation." In 1974 the trial ended and Marshall was sentenced to ten to thirty years in federal prison.

It simply was not in John Stennis's nature to quit or be intimidated by hard times. He simply pressed on. This unconquerable spirit was never more evident than in 1983 and 1984. In August of 1983, the senator's wife succumbed to a long illness stemming from chronic high blood pressure. The senator said of his dearly departed companion, "She always carried her part of the load and was a great help to me." He then added, "She kept her courage up throughout her illness, always serving as a source of encouragement to others." I especially agree with the last part of that statement. Ms. Coy was a dear friend. She was laid to rest in DeKalb.

Yet, even after the loss of his friend and closest confidant, Stennis continued to serve his state and country. In February of 1984, for example, both he and I commended President Reagan for moving United States troops out of Beirut. I told reporters that this move was the type of action that I had been recommending for months. "The U.S. presence will still be strongly felt with our Marines stationed on the ships." I also added, "But the Marines will not be caught in the crossfire of the different warring factions."

For his part, Stennis said that troops should be completely withdrawn from the area. He argued for a "complete withdrawal of all American troops from the region" because, to him, "it was increasingly clear that they cannot keep peace in Lebanon . . .and the risk involved in their presence there is far too great."

The senator faced yet another life-threatening challenge at the conclusion of 1984 when it was discovered that he had cancer. He was again admitted to Walter Reed Hospital. A malignant tumor was found in the upper thigh of his left leg. Because the cancer was so severe, the entire leg had to be removed. But the surgery was a success, and it did stop the cancer. Typical of Stennis's character he awoke the next day and was in very good spirits. He could not, however, use the artificial leg they gave him because he was just too old to make it work. So he used crutches and, in his last days, a wheelchair.

Still, the Senator continued his work in the Senate up until his retirement in 1989. This was a sad day for the state and the country. The outpouring of gratitude for the senator's nearly forty years of service in the Senate was incredible. One of those people expressing gratitude was Democratic Senator Robert Byrd of West Virginia. He talked about how he admired the senator and how he was impressed with the man who "look[ed] like a Senator, talk[ed] like a Senator, should be a Senator and [was] a Senator." Yet, despite his high position, Byrd said that Stennis had "frequently gone out of his way to help and to encourage younger Senators, new Senators." This trait of helping others was indeed an aspect of the senator's personality that everyone admired.

Thad Cochran, the Mississippi Republican senator, also had some very kind words to say about Stennis. Cochran said, "I think as we reflect on Senator Stennis'[s] career, we have to all agree that John Stennis also should be placed among those giants of Mississippi history who have served our State and this Nation in the U.S. Senate." Cochran wrapped up his remarks, saying, "We will certainly miss him, but our best wishes go with him. We know that we will continue to call upon him for his advice and counsel in the months and years ahead."

After he retired from the Senate, Stennis had a house on the

Mississippi State University campus. He was active with the Stennis Center and taught some civics courses. But old age and a sixty-year political career began to take its toll on this public servant. By the early 1990s, his daughter, Margaret Jane, and son, John Hampton, placed the senator in a nursing home in Jackson. I visited with him several times when I was in the area. We would just sit and talk about nothing in particular, but I cherished the time with my close friend.

On April 23, 1995, the senator passed away in his sleep. The friend that I had made at State as a young and ambitious student body president was now gone. We had a friendship that lasted for five decades. I watched his rise in the Senate, and he watched me come into my own in the House. Our friendship, ties to MSU, and dedication to the people of the state had created a strong bond between us.

I spoke of the Senator's death in the House on May 2, 1995. I said, "former Mississippi Senator John C. Stennis died on April 23 at the age of 93. He retired from the Senate in 1989. In the passage of time, we sometimes forget events and accomplishments, but we will not forget Senator Stennis." I went on to summarize his career and said that he was "one of the great statesmen of the twentieth century." I recounted his "courtly southern manner" and "unquestioned integrity and character." But I believed Senator Stennis's career was more than politeness and professionalism. "Senator Stennis was an effective leader who was tough when it came to maintaining a strong national defense and in looking out for his native state. Through more than forty years in the nation's capital, his priority was to put Mississippi first."

As my speech continued, I mentioned the senator's legacy in Mississippi. I noted that his legacy in the state could be seen from the "Tennessee-Tombigbee Waterway in the north, to Meridian's Naval Air Station to the Stennis Space Center on the Gulf Coast." In creating all of these landmarks, he also brought countless jobs and pumped money into the Mississippi economy.

My last few remarks illustrated what John C. Stennis meant to the nation and me. I informed everyone that "in honor of Senator Stennis's commitment to the military, Ronald Reagan announced during his presidency that the Navy's next aircraft carrier would be named the U.S.S. *John C. Stennis*. The ship is undergoing sea trials this spring and summer and will be officially commissioned later this year." I then closed my comments on a more personal note, saying, "Senator Stennis always called me 'his congressman' since I represented his hometown of DeKalb in Kemper County. It was a great honor to serve as his congressman for twenty-eight years and his colleague for twenty-three. He was a remarkable man whose legacy will live on, here in Washington and in his beloved Mississippi."

The Senator was buried in DeKalb, and I served as one of the honorary pallbearers. Over sixty members of Congress and all of the Mississippi congressional members attended the funeral. He was buried next to Ms. Coy. In my opinion, Senator Stennis was one of our greatest senators from Mississippi. He had indeed accomplished what he had set out to do. He had, as a senator, plowed "a straight furrow down to the end of [his] row." For this, and this alone, he was and still is, admired and emulated by those who knew him or have heard of his legendary career as a public servant.

XII

Social Life

I always regretted not being married. I have known many wonderful persons, but it never worked out. I still hope at my age that I would consider marriage if anyone would have me. I think having a family and a loving wife would be the tops in happiness. I notice that those people who have families seem to have more to live for and enjoy life more than others. Being a bachelor is not a bad life, but it seems that having a family could mean more to you and provide a sense of community.

Despite the fact, or perhaps because of the fact, that I came to Congress a bachelor, I was invited to many social functions. Sometimes I was asked to take someone as my date, or I would be asked not to bring anyone so there would be extra men at the event. In Washington, most of the night events are dinner parties and at about a fourth of these dinners there will be an orchestra playing during the dinner, with dancing.

I went to many dinner parties, even though this was not my favorite way to spend an evening. When I first came to Washington, there would be receptions before the dinners that would last for one hour. Then came dinner, which lasted two and a half to three hours. Getting home at midnight and then getting up at 6 A.M. made me pretty tired the next day. I have noticed in the 1990s that the receptions have been reduced to thirty minutes and the salads and desserts are already on the table, which limits the serving time to about thirty minutes, and dinners do not run for three hours.

Over the years I escorted prominent people to different functions before they were married, including such women as Elizabeth Hanford Dole, Polly Bergen, Mary Ann Mobley, Linda Lee Meade, Ava Gabor, Barbara Franklin, and Judy Crowson. Being a bachelor was a key reason I got to know these attractive people. Most of my dates were just good friends, and they moved on to successful careers and happy marriages. I have always remained good friends with all the people I have dated, and we have stayed in touch after going our separate ways. I attended a variety of presidential functions over the years. Several days before July 4, presidents host events on the grounds in back of the White House that face the Washington Monument and other Mall monuments. These are informal events for members of Congress, their families, and other dignitaries. These events usually started around 6 P.M. and would feature well-known entertainers. President Bush liked the Beach Boys and western bands from Texas. He and Barbara also invited me to various functions they held when he was vice president.

Before Christmas, presidents would have Congress members and their families over to see the decorations in the White House.

Each of the rooms on the main floor would be beautifully deco-rated. We would walk through all the rooms, stopping in the main dining room where heavy hors d'oeuvres were served. There were bars providing drinks in designated rooms. In the many years I went to the White House, I never saw a guest or higher government official drinking to excess or even drinking period. In fact, at these and other such events, no one in my observation ever seemed intoxicated. There could be closet drinkers, but I am sure that there is not a heavy drinking problem in the nation's capital.

The staff at the White House does not necessarily change as often as presidents come and go. I knew the staff at the White House, especially when the Bushes were there. I would see some of the same waiters whenever I went to the White House as a member of Congress. President Bush was one of the staff's favorite presidents. He had horseshoe tournaments involving his family and the staff. All the staff enjoyed these tournaments each spring. The president was an excellent player; he developed an effective throw that did not spin the shoe. Our current president, George W. Bush, also likes to pitch horseshoes, and I am told he is having staff tournaments like his father had.

Aside from events at the White House, I also frequently attended functions put on by large organizations from around the country, which came to Washington for various conventions and meetings. I went to most receptions and dinners sponsored by veterans and other military groups. Many of these kinds of events are held on Capitol Hill, which pleased me, as I always liked staying on the Hill for events rather than having to go downtown. There are large rooms on the Hill, like the Cannon Caucus room, and in the Capitol there is the Rotunda.

The veterans' organizations have especially nice affairs in Washington. The V.F.W. used to have a dinner for members of Congress and award high school students from each state that wrote winning essays on patriotism. Because members of Congress did not attend the dinners, the V.F.W. stopped having them and began having receptions from then on for members on the Hill. The American Legion, the Paralyzed Veterans of America, Jewish War Veterans, Amvets, American Prisoners of War, Military Order of the Purple Heart, the Vietnam Veterans of America, and the Blind Veterans Association have for years only had receptions on the Hill. The Disabled American Veterans have their receptions at their headquarters, which is located about five blocks from the Capitol. Those receptions are always nice.

Many Mississippi groups come to Washington and hold receptions, and members of the Mississippi delegation had better show up for those, because they come to see their representatives and senators. Years ago, not too many people from my state had been to the nation's capital. I am proud to say that with better air transportation, many more Mississippians now come here. That is good for them and their representatives. When I first came to Washington in 1967, folks who did come up from Mississippi usually came by car, bus, or train. Now most come by air. I have found that people really enjoy Washington, and there certainly are many attractions to see. Plus, what their representatives do here, along with members from the other states, has a direct impact on their lives.

When George Bush was president, I was always included in whatever social functions he and Barbara had at the White House. Sometimes the president and Barbara would meet me at St. John's Episcopal Church on Lafayette Square, which is across the street from the White House, at 8:00 A.M. for the service, and we would walk back to the White House and have breakfast. When Barbara was out of town, the president would invite me down for supper. President George W. Bush and his wife, Laura, come to St. John's Episcopal Church at Lafayette Square on some Sundays. When they do, they sit in the president's pew and invite me to sit with them. The president was an Episcopalian who switched to his wife's Methodist Church, but they seem to like the services at St. John's.

XIII

Tributes

I have received many honors and tributes during my career, and I would like to share some of those. I am especially proud that during the last session of Congress in which I served, my colleagues named the Department of Veterans Affairs Medical Center in Jackson, Mississippi, in my honor. In the Senate, two of my fellow Mississippians and former fellow House members spoke on behalf of this measure.

Senator Trent Lott made the following comments on September 10, 1996:

Mr. President, I am privileged to have introduced S. 1669, along with Senator Thad Cochran, to name the VA medical center in Jackson, Mississippi, in honor of our friend and colleague, Representative Sonny Montgomery. A companion bill, H.R. 3253, was introduced by Representative Mike Parker, and it has already passed the House.

As many of you know, Congressman Montgomery is retiring at the end of his current term after thirty illustrious years in the House. He has had a distinguished career and served under seven

Presidents. "Mr. Veteran," as many of us have affectionately called Sonny, led efforts to obtain Cabinet-level status for the Department of Veterans Affairs. He introduced and guided to passage a peacetime GI education bill which provides incentives for both recruitment and retention of qualified young men and women for the Armed Forces. This landmark legislation bears his name as the Montgomery GI bill.

Congressman Montgomery has strongly championed the State Veterans Affairs nursing homes. [I must add here that I am proud that there are four such homes in Mississippi now.] He has done yeoman's service for veterans as chairman of the Veterans' Affairs Committee and as a distinguished member of the [House Armed Services Committee]. Veterans throughout the nation have benefited greatly from the outstanding resources provided by VA facilities established and improved under Sonny's watch. In particular, veterans from Mississippi, and neighboring states, are well served by the Veterans Benefits Administration Southern Area Office, the VA Regional Office, and two VA medical centers made possible by the chairman's able hand.

The VA medical center in Jackson definitely needs an official name. Others have distinguished names such as the Sam Rayburn VA, the Jerry Pettis VA, and the James Haley Veterans Hospital. Representative Sonny Montgomery, Congress's "Mr. Veteran," truly is well-deserving of having the Jackson VA Medical Center named in his honor.

It is very appropriate that this legislation comes before us now because of several events that are occurring to pay tribute to Sonny. Representative Montgomery is being honored this week by his colleagues on the House Veterans' Affairs Committee for his dedicated service. Also, Mississippi State University, the chairman's alma mater, is hosting a benefit dinner for him. Proceeds from this benefit will establish the Sonny Montgomery Scholars Program at MSU. Furthermore, House colleagues have made arrangements to plant a magnolia tree on the southeast corner of the Capitol Grounds as a living testimony of Sonny's many years of service and outstanding achievements. [Congressman Pete Geren of Texas, my close friend, did the work and served as master of ceremonies during the ceremony at the tree planting.]

Mr. President, Sonny is one of the most outstanding, revered, and beloved members of Congress. Veterans' Affairs Committee Chairman Alan Simpson is a cosponsor of S. 1669 and strongly supports this measure. I urge my colleagues to join with me in this fitting tribute to our friend and colleague, Representative G. V. (Sonny) Montgomery.

My friend Senator Thad Cochran then arose and made the following statement:

Mr. President, I am pleased to join my colleague in honoring our friend, the gentleman from Mississippi, Sonny Montgomery, who is retiring from the House of Representatives at the end of this Congress. We have joined in sponsoring this bill to name the

VA medical center in Jackson, Mississippi, the G. V. (Sonny) Montgomery Department of Veterans Affairs Medical Center. Throughout his career, as a senior member of the House National Security Committee and as chairman of the Veterans' Affairs Committee, Sonny has demonstrated genuine concern for the health, education, and well-being of our nation's veterans. He firmly believes that we should treat veterans with dignity and compassion, and he has worked hard as chairman of the Veterans' Affairs Committee to enact programs and provide facilities to meet that obligation.

Sonny's concern for and attention to the men and women of our Armed Forces is firmly rooted in his own experiences, having served in the Army and Army National Guard for a total of thirty-eight years. Sonny served in World War II and during the Korean War. As a dedicated member of the Mississippi Army National Guard, he was promoted to the rank of major general before his retirement in 1981.

Sonny's political career began as a member of the Mississippi State Senate from Lauderdale County. He served with distinction for ten years, from 1956 to 1966. [I want to add here a note regarding one of my accomplishments in the state senate that I am quite proud of: I never missed a vote, which was and is a record for that institution.] In 1966, he ran for and won the seat in Congress from the Third District of Mississippi. Sonny has proven to be a very capable, productive, and popular representative. He was overwhelmingly reelected each term since the Ninetieth Congress.

During that thirty-year period of service he has earned the rep-
utation of a champion of national defense and veterans' issues,
and he often is referred to by his colleagues as "Mr. Veteran" or
"Mr. National Guard."

When Sonny was elected to Congress in 1966, American soldiers were fighting in the war in Vietnam. He demonstrated his
concern for those who were involved in that dangerous and
deadly region by spending Christmas each year in Vietnam with
the soldiers.

On these trips, Sonny would carry blank cards with him and
when he ran into young soldiers from Mississippi, he would ask
them to write the names and addresses of their families on these
cards. When Sonny returned home he would take the time to call
each soldier's family to let them know that he had seen their son
or daughter and relay any stories or news that might interest
them. Today, people still thank Sonny for those phone calls.

In 1975 he was appointed chairman of the House Select Committee on Missing Persons in Southeast Asia. In 1977, President
Carter named him to the Woodstock Commission, which traveled to Hanoi to investigate further those Americans missing in
action. More recently, Sonny was a member of the delegation that
brought back the first returned remains of United States personnel missing in North Korea during the Korean War.

Sonny Montgomery stands as an example of a true patriot, and
for this he has been recognized by his colleagues many times. In
1984, the Speaker of the House asked that he lead the House con-

tingent to the commemoration of the fortieth anniversary of the D-day invasion at Normandy, a particularly appropriate designation because Sonny fought in the European theater during this war. In 1988, when the reciting of the Pledge of Allegiance was instituted as daily practice by the House of Representatives, Sonny was asked by the Speaker [Jim Wright of Texas] to be the first Member to lead this body in the Pledge.

Throughout our time together as members of our State's congressional delegation, I have had the opportunity to observe Sonny in many situations. A most recent instance was during the last round of base closure and realignment. Two of the bases in his district were considered for closure, one of which had been on the closure list in two previous rounds. Sonny was most persuasive and successful in convincing the Base Closure Commission that Naval Air Station Meridian and Columbus Air Force Base are essential to the pilot training in both of those services. Sonny was willing to do everything he could to keep these bases open. Today, these bases remain open, largely due to the efforts of Sonny Montgomery.

As a senior member of the House Armed Services Committee . . . Sonny Montgomery has been a tremendous influence on our national defense policy. He has consistently supported the maintenance of a strong force.

Sonny was one of only seven Democrats who in early 1994 paid a visit to President Clinton to insist on increased defense spending by his administration, particularly in the area of military pay, and to urge him to reduce non-defense spending. . . . Sonny has always considered the protection of our freedom to be the highest priority of our Government, and he has done his best to ensure our national security.

Because of Sonny Montgomery, the National Guard and Reserves are different services than they were twenty-five years ago. As a member of the Mississippi Army National Guard Sonny saw untapped potential in the Guard and Reserve forces, and as a senior member of the . . . [Armed Services Committee], he has strengthened our reserve component forces in significant ways. Over and over again, Sonny insisted that in order for the Guard and Reserves to be truly ready reserve forces, they must have first-line equipment, top facilities, and more serious training. As we saw in the Gulf War, our Guard and Reserves have now been transformed into an essential component of our total forces. In addition, Sonny has always emphasized the need to keep the missions of each Guard unit relevant.

Recently, Sonny negotiated with officials at the Pentagon in order to reassign the duties of a National Guard battalion in east Mississippi, which might have been considered for closure. Instead, this battalion will be the first Guard unit in the Nation to be equipped with and train on the high-technology Avenger air defense system, a key weapon in Operations Desert Shield and Desert Storm. Our active forces will be better supported by contributions from National Guard units in the future because of Sonny Montgomery.

Another high priority for him has been the recruitment and retention of soldiers; and out of this concern came the GI bill which bears his name. Sonny considers this legislation to be his greatest accomplishment. Under the Montgomery GI bill, active duty, National Guard, and Reserve personnel are entitled to educational assistance benefits which would enable them to pursue their educational goals while serving our country. Since being passed into law in 1985, approximately 2 million military personnel have participated in the program, and over 500,000 have already attended schools with its assistance. The Montgomery GI bill has significantly improved recruiting efforts for all of the services, and it has provided much-needed training to veterans and retirees preparing to enter the workforce. [I might add here that it has been said by military officials that the GI Bill is the best recruiting and retention tool that the military has.]

In addition to protecting our national security, Sonny has consistently sought proper recognition and benefits for veterans. In the 100th Congress, Sonny fought [along with Gerry Solomon of New York] to have the Secretary of Veterans Affairs elevated to a Cabinet-level position. When Sonny saw a need to improve the review of veterans' claims, he sponsored a bill to establish the Court of Veterans' Appeals in order to ensure the complete judicial review of each claim. Within a month, this bill was signed into law, and right away veterans saw needed changes in the claims process. Also, he has worked to streamline the services offered at regional service centers and hospitals, aiming toward providing, in effect, one-stop shopping for our veterans.

During the last Congress, Sonny authored legislation to extend compensation to our most recent veterans, those who fought in the Persian Gulf War. The Veterans' Persian Gulf War Benefits Act, now law, requires the VA to give priority to veterans suffering from undiagnosed illnesses after their service in the Persian Gulf region. The bill also established new research and outreach programs to further the identification of this disease. This legislation is just another demonstration of his belief that we have a moral obligation to care for and compensate those who have suffered disabling injuries during their service to our country.

While in the Army and for his efforts in service to military personnel and veterans of our country, Sonny has received many awards, including the Legion of Merit, Meritorious Service Medal, Combat Infantry Badge, Army Commendation Medal, a Bronze Star for Valor, and Mississippi Magnolia Cross Award, and the Harry S. Truman Award, which is the highest award given by the National Guard Association of the United States. In addition, he has been recognized by the American Red Cross, the Veterans of Foreign Wars, the Reserve Officers Association of the United States, and AMVETS of World War II. He is past president of the Mississippi National Guard Association, and he remains an active member of the American Legion and VFW Post 79 in

Meridian, Mississippi. Veterans' organizations across the country are saddened to see Sonny retire.

Above all of Sonny's legislative accomplishments, he must be recognized and appreciated for his patience, congeniality, and compassion. Having maintained so many friendships in both parties, Sonny has often been called to be a mediator. He has been on good terms with Republican and Democrat leaders in Congress and presidents of both parties throughout four decades, and his friendship with former President Bush goes back to their days as freshmen in the House. His peers regard him as a respected friend, who is wholly dedicated to his purpose in office. A small example of his loyalty is evidenced by the number of hours he has logged in the speaker's chair, a duty many consider drudgery, but something that Sonny has viewed as an opportunity to serve his fellow Members.

I will miss his good counsel and true friendship, Mississippi's Third District and the entire nation will miss his strong leadership and clear vision. Members like Sonny are rare, and his leaving signals the end of an era for southern Democrats, and the House of Representatives as well.

I am pleased to join my colleague, Senator Lott, in offering S. 1669, a bill to name the Department of Veterans Affairs Medical Center in Jackson, Mississippi, for Sonny Montgomery, and I urge all of my colleagues to support the renaming of this facility.

The next speaker on behalf of this bill was Senator Alan Simpson of Wyoming who added some special remarks that I most appreciated:

> Mr. President, in reflecting on my own lifetime of public service, I can think of no one whose sincere dedication to veterans, combined with the ability to transform that dedication into a concrete reality, exceeds that of my old and dear friend G. V. "Sonny" Montgomery.
>
> We all know why the Montgomery GI bill carries Sonny Montgomery's name. It's not just an honor, it is a clear depiction of reality. What some members of this body may not realize is that Sonny Montgomery's interests and everlasting impact extend far beyond the veterans' education benefit that carries his name.
>
> There is no path down which a veteran may travel that hasn't been scouted first and smoothed and improved by the congressman from Mississippi, Sonny Montgomery.
>
> There is no benefit provided to our veterans by a grateful nation that does not bear the imprint of the longtime chairman, and now ranking minority member, of the House Committee on Veterans' Affairs, Sonny Montgomery.
>
> The rules of the Senate Committee on Veterans' Affairs limit proposals to name VA facilities to the names of individuals who are deceased. As we consider the measure before us today, some may wonder what has occurred to amend that standard.
>
> If such a person were to exist, I could assume that they do not know the stirring thirty-year record of service and legislation

written by Sonny Montgomery. If such a question is raised, I will only say to the inquirer that exceptional service calls for exceptional action and that such an action also calls for an exception to the rule. This is such a time. A rule that would prohibit application of the name G. V. Sonny Montgomery to the VA Medical Center in Jackson, Mississippi, is a rule begging to be temporarily laid aside—in sheer gratitude from us all.

In fact, Sonny Montgomery is the dominant presence in the world of veterans' affairs, and the genial and generous shadow he casts extends far beyond the boundaries of the State of Mississippi. An honor limited only to his native State of Mississippi is an honor quite inadequate to describe his full legacy.

In reflecting on the full and honest career and commitment of the senior congressman from Mississippi, I conclude that if honors truly reflected accomplishment, we would likely have to name the whole shooting match of the Department of Veterans Affairs after Sonny Montgomery.

When Sonny Montgomery leaves us in the Congress and returns to his beloved home as a private citizen he will leave behind an unmatched legacy of unselfish service. He will leave behind shoes that it would take a giant to fill. The only way that veterans may not benefit in the future from the career of Sonny Montgomery will be if the height of the bar he set is up there so high that those who follow him may be discouraged by the fact that it will be so difficult to equal, much less exceed, his remarkable records. Sonny Montgomery will serve as an example to generations of all legislators to come. I am so very proud to join in supporting legislation to recognize an example, and a career, and a wonderful, never tiring, ever focused, lovely, kind, incomparable man, by ensuring that the VA Medical Center in Jackson, Mississippi, will forever carry the name that his actions have made synonymous with love of veterans: G. V. Sonny Montgomery.

I love him. He has saved my skin a time or two. He is my true friend. God bless him.

Such comments from good friends are to me the most valuable fruits of a career in public service. In addition to these statements that were entered into the *Congressional Record*, I received many personal notes and letters after I announced that I would not seek reelection. I would like to share some of those, too.

Dave Gribbin, at the time a member of Indiana Senator Dan Coats's staff, sent the following: "I learned a lot by working with and watching you. I'll never forget when I was in the Pentagon and we decided we wanted to reduce Guard and Reserve . . . strength. I worked it hard, and assured Secretary [Dick] Cheney that we were making progress. On the day of the vote on the Floor, about noon, I could feel the tide turn. Votes for our position began disappearing like mist in the sun. We lost big. What happened, I asked. The answer was a one word reply . . . 'Sonny.' I wish you the best as you move ahead. You can rest assured that you made an *enormous* difference for good during your stay in this town."

From Norm Busch, VFW commander of Illinois, came these words: "On behalf of the 107,000 members of the Veterans of Foreign Wars in the Department of Illinois, please allow me to convey to you, our sincere appreciation for your untiring efforts on behalf of veterans nationwide. We know we have lost a true friend. We would like to wish you the very best in your retirement and to thank you once again for all that you have done for veterans throughout your many years of service."

An old acquaintance from the Reagan years, Casper "Cap" Weinberger, responded to news of my retirement: "I was sorry indeed to read of your decision to leave the Congress next year, but can of course completely understand it. However, I could not let the event pass without writing to tell you how deeply I have appreciated not only your many personal kindnesses and friendship to me, but the really great service you have performed for the country. As I am sure you will recall in 1980 the public, and some in the Congress, were failing signally in their response to honor and support the men and women who fight for us. You were always a strong, clear voice for the kind of legislation and the kind of moral support that our troops need. I was deeply grateful to you then and am still."

Several members of the House had nice things to say. Pat Schroeder of Colorado said: "I can't deal with your retirement.

You've been my buddy too long! You're NOT allowed to leave. I thought you had to get written permission from me first!" From Saxby Chambliss of Georgia: "I was sorry to hear the news of your retirement while I was home last week. You are one of the most reassuring things I have found in congress. Your honesty, your statesmanship, your commitment to your country & your love of God will be sorely missed." From Tim Roemer of Indiana: "Your efforts and contributions on behalf of our Nation's veterans such as the 'G.I. bill' are exceptional, and I am particularly grateful for your leadership and active support for federal programs such as the HMMWV facility in Mishawaka and the activities of the Army Reserves and National Guard, which are of critical importance to Indiana's Third Congressional District. Your participation in the Elkhart veterans' town meeting in 1992 is a shining example of your tireless commitment to military retirees across the country. I am confident that your endeavors following your service in Congress will be as valuable to those with whom you work and seek to assist, and I sincerely hope that they prove enjoyable and rewarding to you." From Barbara Mikulski of Maryland: "It was with a tinge of sadness that I read of your resignation from an institution you have loved and served well for so many years. Veterans will lose a strong advocate and I will lose a dear colleague. You will leave your mark on Congress as the General who guarded the gate, who stood sentry for our veterans, who watched over the programs which helped make their lives so much better." From Stephen Horn of California: "I was saddened to learn of your retirement. You are a great legislative role-model. When I was serving as a professor of political science and teaching a course on Congress prior to my election, I used your use of the Suspense Calendar as an example of a confident, effective legislator who knew how to avoid the Committee on Rules. We will miss you!" From Ron Klink of Pennsylvania: "I was very dismayed to hear that you've decided to retire. It has been a great pleasure to know you and serve with you these past years. You can leave knowing that your many years of service will long be remembered and appreciated by those you've served. The veterans never will have a greater friend or champion than Chairman Montgomery!"

I received a brief but treasured card from a man I admire very much. He has been strong for our country during past crises, like Desert Storm, and he is now standing tall as secretary of defense in our nation's war against terrorism. General Colin Powell wrote: "Dear Sonny, I can't believe it! Remember to turn out the lights when you leave. Sonny, you're the greatest and amassed a remarkable record of service to the troops and the nation. I will always remember with fondest memories our jousts."

An old and trusted friend, Monty Spear, whom I worked with on the MIA/POW issue, wrote: "It was with regret that I read the recent announcement of your retirement in the press. I know what a long and distinguished career you have had in the Congress and all you have done for our country's defense and its veterans, in particular. I count my time with your Select Committee on POWs and MIAs in Southeast Asia as one of the high points in my own career. You were willing to take responsibility for discovering unpleasant facts and telling the truth about them, even at the risk of being unpopular. My regret at your retirement is tempered by the thought that you will now be able to do the things *you* want to do, at your own pace."

Joe Vokey, at the time commander of the Department of Maine VFW, wrote me a gracious letter: "It is with mixed emotions that I am writing you on the behalf of the members of the Great State of Maine, Veterans of Foreign Wars. Congratulations upon your impending retirement. I have to tell you that this is like the I.R.S. going over a cliff in my brand new Lincoln. We are pleased with your ability to retire; but, we have also lost a great friend in the House of Representatives. All veterans in this country owe you a tremendous debt of gratitude. Your untiring efforts to expand, protect, and support veteran issues will be sorely missed. As you enter retirement, I will have the pleasure of knowing that I have personally met you at our Washington Conference and that you are a great gentleman, statesman, and a sincere friend of all veterans. The Montgomery G.I. Bill was a major achievement; but, all veterans are aware of your constant support of Defense and VA benefit issues. As you enter retirement, you can take with you the knowledge of a 'Job Well Done.' May you have 'fair winds and following seas' in whatever you do."

John B. Conaway, retired lieutenant general and former chief of the National Guard Bureau wrote a fine letter to my home state newspaper, the *Jackson Clarion-Ledger*: "I know Mississippi and all its fine citizens are proud of 3rd District U.S. Rep. G. V. 'Sonny' Montgomery. He is a most humble man and one of those rare public servants who graces us with his tireless efforts to always help his constituents and all of America. I am most thankful that Congressman Montgomery came my way. We are all saddened by his announcement not to seek reelection in 1996. I personally understand because of the great devotion to serving and the long hours he puts in seven days a week always trying to make America a better place to live and work. After many years of service in the military, to community and state and 30 years in the U.S. House of Representatives, he truly has earned his upcoming retirement at the end of 1996. I have worked closely with Mr. Montgomery the last 18 years during my tenure in the National Guard Bureau at the Pentagon. Sonny has become my closest friend in the U.S. Congress. He has never forgotten his roots in Mississippi, the people, his friends, our military, the National Guard, reserve and veterans. He works tirelessly to enhance the readiness and modernization of our forces as the primary backup tour active components. On the floor of the House, he is also called the 'General' and known as 'Mr. National Guard' in Congress. He will always be known as the Father of the modern day 'Montgomery G.I. Bill.' Already, more than 2 million men and women of the active, guard, and reserve forces have taken advantage of this great program to further their education to 'add value to America.' It has also become the No. 1 recruiting tool for our military. Sonny is what we in the National Guard call 'America at its best.' God is good for sending Sonny Montgomery our way. We will miss his strong voice in Congress in 1997, but all can rest assured he will continue to be a strong advocate for Mississippi, the military and the veterans."

Speaking of the largest newspaper in my home state, the *Clarion-Ledger*, on October 4, 1995, the paper editorialized about my retirement in a way that made me feel very good. I always treasured the support of my state, not only from the people in my district but also from warm-hearted Mississippians in all parts of the state. The editorial was as follows: "The announcement that 3rd District U.S. Rep. G. V. 'Sonny' Montgomery will not seek another term in Congress is a sad one. But the conservative Democrat from Meridian deserves admiration and best wishes as he makes this move. First elected to Congress in 1966, after 10 years in the Mississippi Senate, Congressman Montgomery earned a devoted following of constituents. His district has varied widely over the years, but with everyone he has sought to represent their interests well. Never one to seek the limelight, he went about helping others, trying to meet their needs. He took many pains to be accessible, which endeared him to many. Montgomery's forte was veterans' affairs. That is understandable. So many people know Montgomery as congressman, but he was a military leader as well. He is a retired major general in the Mississippi National Guard. He won more awards for valor and service in World War II and the Korean War than can easily be named—including the Bronze Star. The G.I. Bill that helps service personnel go to college is named for him. During the Reagan administration, Montgomery achieved tremendous power as a leader among the so-called 'boll weevils,' a group of mostly Southern conservative Democrats. They served as key swing votes between the then-Democrat-controlled Congress and the Republican administration of President Reagan. Montgomery is a friend of former President Bush, too. Mississippi has been fortunate to have had powerful members of Congress, with influence far greater than the population of the state would normally gain. Montgomery is among the most influential to have served The Magnolia State, but his personality, his quiet bearing, his courtly manners and down-home friendliness never failed him. Mississippi has gained greatly to have Gillespie V. 'Sonny' Montgomery for nearly 30 years in Congress. He was a friend to legions and an inspiration, too. In retirement, we wish him well."

Herbert Williams, a retired military veteran, who at the time lived in Biloxi, Mississippi, wrote a lengthy letter to me in which he made some special comments that really touched me. I share here excerpts from his statements:

> None of us can go on forever. We knew you stayed on because we and the country have a special place in your heart, mind, and respect as you [do] ours. It wasn't the esteemed position and power you possessed that kept you on—it was your desire to help the nation and us as long as possible. You have made history and

history has a special place for you. Your name is legend among
the nation, veterans, retirees and annuitants. You have earned the
respect of all. You have carved with honor and compassion your
niche in life, history, and our hearts and minds by honest labor,
always looking out for us and the nation. Your niche was also
carved with the milk of human kindness, caring, honest Christian labor, devotion to duty, honor, and country. We do not know
of anyone currently who can replace you without extensive on-
the-job training. There are very few combat leaders who really
understand 'Old time' veterans and service retirees. You understand what we went through and where we have been. You understand our moods, how we think, write, and act. You understand
our rages and are able to bring tranquility from the chaos we can
so aptly create at times. You reason with us when we are unrea-
sonable. You can guide us down the correct path when we get
'bent out of shape.' When we are right you will go to bat and stand
up for us. When we are wrong you do not chastise us but merely
point the way to progress. You talk to us straight when we cannot
understand the administration and they cannot understand us.
You are a buffer between those of us whose motto was not just
'follow me' but 'lead, follow, or get the hell out of the way.' You
have a way with us that no leader today can understand . . . You
can elevate us when we are down and settle us down when we get
flying off the deep end. . . .You are the 'soldier's soldier,' the 'airman's airman,' the 'sailor's sailor,' the 'marine's marine,' the 'legislator's legislator,' the 'man's man.' . . . The great leaders of your

stature [and] caliber are gone. Compassion and caring for those that have borne the brunt of battle and are retired, old, in financial stress, and those needing extensive medical care in their waning years have disappeared. . . . The cloak of responsibility and duty weighed heavy on your shoulders. You were not wrapped up in your own importance. Most of all was your realization that the wants of the country could not be carried out without the respect and reverence of those serving with you whether in the military or congress. . . . I could easily get thousands upon thousands of signatures to this tribute. I speak for all. Those who made the supreme sacrifice resting in hallowed ground in our country, far away and in foreign lands, the aged, the home-bound, the surviving families, residents of the veterans hospitals, nursing homes, those too infirm to write, those too unaware to know.

I think that the words of this veteran speak volumes as to why I dedicated myself to their welfare. Those who sacrifice for their country have a right to expect their country to be there for them. I did my best to see that our country lived up to those expectations.

A man I admired very much, Dr. William L. Giles, a former president of my alma mater, Mississippi State University, sent me a nice personal note that I want to share: "Thank you for your many years of dedicated public service. You have done great things for the state of Mississippi and Mississippi State. I admire you for your humility, your ability to get things done and the favorable impression you have made for your State in the halls of Congress. You will be missed when you retire. Your effectiveness in dealing with the leaders in our nation will not soon be replaced. On the other hand, I admire you for stepping down while you are still active. I hope you have many years ahead to enjoy life."

Another longtime ally and personal friend, David "Boo" Ferris of Cleveland, contacted me. Boo was an outstanding major league baseball player with the Boston Red Sox and an outstanding coach at Delta State University in Cleveland, Mississippi. In his letter, Boo said, "I want to congratulate you and commend you on a great and distinguished career in Congress. The outstanding service you have rendered your state and nation is immeasurable, and your accomplishments will continue to pay dividends in years to come. You have done so much for so many, always having a sincere interest and concern for the people you serve. I am proud for you and your successes. Be assured I treasure our wonderful friendship that began when we enrolled as freshmen at Mississippi State in 1939, and I continue to appreciate your many kindnesses to me through the years."

My close friend, President George Bush, who wrote a special foreword for this volume, also wrote upon the occasion of my retirement a wonderful tribute to me, which was distributed in Mississippi. I cherish it very much and wish to share it here:

Yesterday my dear personal friend, Sonny Montgomery, announced that he would not seek another term. I write simply to express my high regard for Sonny. Admittedly I am not an objective observer, because he is the closest personal friend I ever had in the House of Representatives. Congressman Montgomery never forgot who sent him to Congress. He has always voted his district, often standing up against enormous pressure from his own party to do just that. He was never afraid to vote with the Republicans when he felt they were right, to oppose them when he felt they were wrong. When I was President, I counted on Sonny for his advice and wise counsel. I called on him a lot. He never let me down. Our friendship was (and is) that strong. And when I was hurting a little or when tensions were really high, I'd call him up. He would come down to the White House to help out his old friend—to lift me up and give me strength. He was always kind and considerate to my family, long before I became President, too. We Bushes respect your Congressman; and the truth is we love the guy, too. He will be missed by the people of his district; and his sensible conservative voice will be missed by the country, too.

My old and dear friend Henry "Hank" Moseley, a retired Air Force colonel and fellow Mississippian, wrote a letter of tribute to the *Starkville Daily News*, that was published on October 31, 1995. I told him that of all the tributes that I had received, his was the most glowing and meant the most to me. I felt that way then and still do. And ole Hank is still going strong, serving as a local representative for Congressman Chip Pickering, my successor. Here are Hank's words:

For the past 30 years, the people of the 3rd Congressional District have enjoyed and experienced unparalleled leadership by its Congressman G. V. "Sonny" Montgomery. We have had a lawmaker on the Potomac that has been vitally concerned about his constituents, and has worked extremely hard to translate that concern into action. You don't have to look very far in any direction in our District, State or Nation, to see his help and work in making life better for all residents regardless of race, color or creed. Nationally, you hear of his untiring efforts to support Defense, the Veterans and the National Guard. That support has been tremendous, but I am here to tell you from first hand knowledge that his work with local governments, communities, and the people in the 3rd District should not be overlooked. A close check will find that he frequently visits the District to find out the problems, and then applies himself diligently in trying to solve them. Further, you will find that "Sonny" has been equally instrumental in securing grants for water associations, airport improvements, support for education, community development and providing a "constituent service" second to none. One thing that I have learned from my association with "Sonny" is that you never get ahead of him, because he carries a little black book and is adept at recording contacts and following up to make sure promises are fulfilled. In my opinion the hallmark of "Sonny"'s success is: commitment, dedication, loyalty and a staff fully in sync with his goals and objectives. This translates into statesmanship. My friendship with "Sonny" extends over many, many years, and began with our common love for Mississippi State University. During this time, I have seen him move from being a successful insurance broker to the Mississippi Senate, and subsequently to the U.S. Congress. I was at his swearing-in-ceremony in January 1967, and recall how proud he was to be representing the people of the 3rd District. Since his swearing-in, he has never let any grass grow under his feet in working for his constituency and his state. He has been an outward spokesman for strong family values and high moral principles. His loyalty, integrity, dedication, and compassion to his fellow man is unquestionable. Yes, he is a true leader and statesman of whom we can all be justifiably proud. As our "Man on the Potomac" begins his countdown to retirement in January 1997, I know all residents of the District, the State, and the Nation, join me in thanking him for a job well done.

Over the years, I have kept in close touch with my beloved alma mater, Mississippi State University. I have always offered my assistance to MSU, and of course I am delighted that my congressional papers are located in the Congressional and Political Research Center in the university library. I have many friends there, and I would like to share the comments of a former MSU president, Donald Zacharias. Dr. Zacharias and I have had a wonderful relationship over the years, and I appreciate his writing the following:

Representative Sonny Montgomery is an alumnus who was serving the U.S. House of Representatives when I first met him. His attitude when I became acquainted with him was one of wanting to know what he could do to be helpful to the students, faculty, and staff at the university. He realized that he was serving some of the most creative and hardworking people in the country, and they were all in his congressional district.

He and I often talked about commencement and other ceremonial events at the university. We reviewed its importance to our students and their families and what a contribution an outstanding speaker could make to that occasion. With his help Elizabeth Dole became one of our speakers and impressed the crowd with her ability to motivate and with her personal respect for Congressman Montgomery.

A few years later he informed us that he believed that President George Bush would address our graduates if we wished. Our commencement planners expressed a strong desire to have the President come to Starkville and Sonny extended the invitation on behalf of the university. The responding crowd for commencement was so large that the event was held in the football arena. President Bush made it clear that he came because of his great respect for our alumnus, Sonny Montgomery.

Regardless of the issues before the Congress, Representative Montgomery was ready to help. He came to the campus often to keep in touch with the needs and atmosphere of Mississippi State. From the Agriculture Division's Homecoming breakfast to formal dinners in the home of the university president, he was always willing to assist if his presence was needed. He also made it clear that he was on campus because of his desire to serve the people of Mississippi. It was never for personal recognition or to impress anyone with his position. He wanted to help life to be better for the people he served.

I enjoyed being his friend and quickly learned that he chose to be of the greatest service possible to the people of the university. He displayed that same commitment to the people of America throughout his professional career.

I have shared these, just a few of the tributes and compliments I received at the end of my congressional year, to demonstrate what a rich, full life public service can bring. The many friendships I have enjoyed have brought me much joy over the years, and I am glad that I can point with pride to solid friendships I have with congressional colleagues on both sides of the aisle and from the a broad spectrum of political philosophies. No matter how strongly I might disagree with fellow congressmen, I tried never to let those disagreements translate into any kind of personal animosity. To be effective, Congress must have an air of collegiality, and unfortunately I do not think that kind of respect exists as much now as it did during my congressional years. I hope it returns. The terrorist-induced tragedies we have faced recently seemed to inspire a return, and we should all hope it lasts. We must all work together to get things done.

As most of the testimonials above show, my proudest legacy is the role I have played in expanding and protecting the rights and governmental support of our veterans. Also, I hope that my career inspires young people to be actively involved in public and political activities and perhaps seek elective office. I have given my personal and congressional papers to the Congressional and Political Research Center in the Mississippi State University Library, and I have set up scholarship funds at MSU in order not only to encourage scholarly research but to inspire future generations of young people to be active American citizens, no matter what road they may go down. I have been blessed, and as I pass the torch, may God richly bless those who pick up that torch and keep America great.

INDEX